Universities and elites in Britain since 1800

# New Studies in Economic and Social History

*Edited for the Economic History Society by*
Michael Sanderson
*University of East Anglia, Norwich*

This series, specially commissioned by the Economic History Society, provides a guide to the current interpretations of the key themes of economic and social history in which advances have recently been made or in which there has been significant debate.

In recent times economic and social history has been one of the most flourishing areas of historical study. This has mirrored the increasing relevance of the economic and social sciences both in a student's choice of career and in forming a society at large more aware of the importance of these issues in their everyday lives. Moreover specialist interests in business, agricultural and welfare history, for example, have themselves burgeoned and there has been an increased interest in the economic development of the wider world. Stimulating as these scholarly developments have been for the specialist, the rapid advance of the subject and the quantity of new publications make it difficult for the reader to gain an overview of particular topics, let alone the whole field.

*New Studies in Economic and Social History* is intended for students and their teachers. It is designed to introduce them to fresh topics and to enable them to keep abreast of recent writing and debates. All the books in the series are written by a recognised authority in the subject, and the arguments and issues are set out in a critical but unpartisan fashion. The aim of the series is to survey the current state of scholarship, rather than to provide a set of prepackaged conclusions.

The series has been edited since its inception in 1968 by Professors M. W. Flinn, T. C. Smout and L. A. Clarkson, and is currently edited by Dr Michael Sanderson. From 1968 it was published by Macmillan as *Studies in Economic History*, and after 1974 as *Studies in Economic and Social History*. From 1995 *New Studies in Economic and Social History* is being published on behalf of the Economic History Society by Cambridge University Press. This new series includes some of the titles previously published by Macmillan as well as new titles, and reflects the ongoing development throughout the world of this rich seam of history.

*For a full list of titles in print, please see the end of the book.*

# Universities and elites in Britain since 1800

*Prepared for the Economic History Society by*

## R. D. Anderson
*University of Edinburgh*

CAMBRIDGE
UNIVERSITY PRESS

Published by the Press Syndicate of the University of Cambridge
The Pitt Building, Trumpington Street, Cambridge CB2 1RP
40 West 20th Street, New York, NY 10011-4211, USA
10 Stamford Road, Oakleigh, Melbourne 3166, Australia

*Universities and Elites in Britain since 1800* first published by
The Macmillan Press Limited 1992
First Cambridge University Press edition 1995

Printed in Great Britain at the University Press, Cambridge

*A catalogue record for this book is available from the British Library*

*Library of Congress cataloguing in publication data applied for*


ISBN 0 521 55275 3 hardback
ISBN 0 521 55778 X paperback

# Contents

# Tables

# Note on references

References within square brackets relate to the numbered items in the Bibliography; where page numbers are given, they are printed in italics, for example [76, *231*].

# Acknowledgements

Work on this book began in the scholarly and hospitable atmosphere of the Center for Studies in Higher Education at the University of California, Berkeley, and I am grateful to the Center and its acting director, Sheldon Rothblatt, for their support.

Others who have helped in various ways include Paul Addison, Laurence Brockliss, Jennifer Carter, Owen Dudley Edwards, Daniel Greenstein, Jan Rupp and Donald Withrington.

Any errors are, of course, my own responsibility

# Introduction

University history long took the form of histories of individual institutions, often of a celebratory and inward-looking kind, and it was not until the 1950s that historians tried to look at the modern university system as a whole. Since then a solid body of work has been built up by scholars like A. J. Engel, Roy Lowe, Sheldon Rothblatt and Michael Sanderson. The present study seeks to explore some of the implications of their work, and to relate university history to the general social history of modern Britain. In recent years, a new dimension has been added by comparative studies: books like Fritz Ringer's *Education and Society in Modern Europe* [105] or the collective volumes by various historians on *The Transformation of Higher Learning 1860–1930* [63] and *The Rise of the Modern Educational System* [92] place Britain in an international context.

These historians have identified three stages of long-term development, called by Ringer the early, high and late industrial phases. In the first phase, universities continued their traditional task of serving the older landed and professional élite. In the second, starting around 1860, they began to adapt to the needs of industrial society, particularly by training the growing professions. Between the 1860s and the 1930s, see Jarausch, there was a 'seismic shift' by which 'a small, homogeneous, elite and pre-professional university turned into a large, diversified, middle-class and professional system of higher learning' [63, *10*]. There was a substantial increase of student numbers, and in this formative period redefinition of the university's social role coincided with the establishment of the 'research ideal', combining scholarship and teaching under the direction of an autonomous academic profession. 'Professional-

ization', a process traced for England in important books by
Harold Perkin [95; 97], has commonly been seen as the motive
force of university expansion, and the professional ethos was linked
with ideas of culture and 'liberal' education. Ringer and others
have pointed to the incongruence between the curriculum inspired
by this ideal and the values of an industrial entrepreneurial society.
Universities, it is alleged, failed to serve the direct needs of the
economy, and encouraged the middle classes to identify themselves with 'aristocratic' ideals.

The Victorian period saw a natural expansion of élite education
as middle-class occupations grew. In Ringer's terms, education
became more 'inclusive'; but it did not necessarily become more
'progressive' – i.e. include more students from lower social groups.
Although education never lost its association with social mobility,
and some poor but talented boys always reached universities, it has
been argued that in the nineteenth century the ambitious and
competitive middle classes took over these institutions for their
own purposes and excluded many who might previously have
benefited. Hartmut Kaelble, using another three-phase scheme,
has identified periods of 'charitable', 'competitive' and 'welfare'
opportunities, and he sees equality of opportunity increasing only
in the third phase of expansion, with the rise of the welfare state
and deliberate policies of democratization [68].

Another organizing concept is 'systematization': as education
became more widely available, it is said, the system became more
complex, hierarchical and 'segmented' (Ringer's term). The social
effects of expansion were blunted, and existing privileges defended,
by diverting new demands into alternative channels with less
prestige. Two British peculiarities are especially relevant here: the
dominance of Oxford and Cambridge (for which the abbreviation
'Oxbridge' is too convenient to avoid, though it may conceal
differences between the two), and the privileged position of the
English 'public schools' as roads to university education and to
élite positions generally.

One aim of this study is to test ideas about élite formation, the
restriction or expansion of opportunity, and the nature of the
British educational hierarchy. But there are some topics which
current historical approaches, with their emphasis on class, occupation and social mobility, sometimes neglect. One is gender, for

the admission of women to universities in the late nineteenth century and their subsequent progress is one of the most striking features of recent history. Another is religion, the focus of some of the most bitter debates in the past. And the third is the different educational traditions within the British Isles. With a few exceptions (notably the work of Sanderson) generalization about Britain takes an English standpoint, and fails to take full account of the university history of Scotland, Wales and Ireland. Chapter One will outline the development of a 'system' with particular reference to England, but Chapter Two will endeavour to do justice to national diversity. Chapter Three will consider the relationship between universities and élite values, including the much debated question of whether education has contributed to the decline of the British economy. Chapter Four will look more closely at the social function of universities in the 'high industrial' phase, particularly their connexion with the professions and the social structure, while Chapter Five will ask whether the changes of the twentieth century have been as effective as was hoped in widening educational opportunity.

The theme of 'élites' has been chosen as a common thread in these debates, and is used fairly loosely, to mean not just the small 'governing' élite, or the top decision-makers in the various areas of national life, but all those who occupied positions of relative wealth and influence, whether in the professions, the public service or business. When looking at the English provinces or the non-English nations we shall ask how far such people derived a distinctive system of values from their education, and when discussing educational opportunity we shall start from the assumption that the admission of new social groups to higher education represents a widening of élite recruitment.

# 1
# The growth of a system

The notion of three phases of long-term development in higher education is a useful starting-point, provided that chronological subdivisions are also allowed for. The first phase may be seen as lasting until the 1870s, the second from then until the 1950s. The first phase was 'traditional', in that the demand for university education remained limited, but it also saw innovations: the foundation of modern rivals to Oxford and Cambridge, from around 1830, and the reform of the ancient universities them-selves, which gathered speed from 1850. By the 1870s Oxford and Cambridge had been modernized and launched on a new career of success, and the foundation of 'civic' universities in English provincial cities led to rapid expansion of numbers. By 1889 the state was prepared to intervene with subsidies, and by 1914 there was something like a national university system. The Scottish universities, which had previously gone their own way, took large steps towards assimilation, and university education was founded in Wales. By 1914, too, deliberate if limited policies of equality of opportunity were being pursued. The First World War had significant effects on student numbers, but the inter-war period was one of stagnation, and it took another war to stimulate further expansion. This took off in the 1950s and 1960s, and inaugurated a third phase in which universities had to share their position with other institutions, and in which participation reached levels which pointed to, if they have not yet reached, the qualitative shift from élite to mass higher education.

Few countries have had universities as confined to the élite as England in 1800, and the new century was unlikely to leave Oxford and Cambridge untouched. While most European universities (including the Scottish ones) combined general education with vocational preparation for the professions or the bureaucracy, Oxford and Cambridge had turned their backs on professional education, and offered a narrow curriculum based on classics at Oxford and mathematics at Cambridge. Their students were sons either of the aristocracy and gentry, for whom the university was a social finishing school as much as an intellectual experience, or of the clergy. So far as the universities had a vocational task, it was to supply the clergy of the Church of England, of which they were an integral part. There were religious tests which confined their benefits to anglicans, and most of the teachers were in clerical orders.

These features, and the heavy expense required by an aristocratic lifestyle based on residential colleges, made the universities largely irrelevant to the needs of the new middle classes, many of whom were nonconformist. There was a demand, if a limited one, for cheaper and more modern alternatives, and around 1830 this coincided with utilitarian attacks on Oxford and Cambridge as corrupt corporations misusing resources which ought to belong to the whole nation. If the English bourgeoisie had been stronger, they might have taken the universities over and reformed them in their own image to form a new, modern élite recruited on principles of talent and merit rather than birth and privilege, as happened in France after the revolution [145]. But in England the landed and anglican establishment was too powerful, and early attempts to open up Oxbridge failed. The alternative strategy was to found new colleges, and the first appeared as the 'University of London' in 1828. It was renamed University College London (UCL) in 1836, when a new University of London was founded to grant degrees to its students and those of King's College London, opened in 1831 as an anglican riposte.

UCL and Owens College Manchester, founded in 1851, are usually seen as the most significant developments of this period, both being non-denominational, and offering new subjects not available in the fossilized Oxbridge curricula. Manchester was, after all, the symbolic capital of the provincial, entrepreneurial, nonconformist middle class. However, while it is convenient to see nonconformity as a kind of ideological expression of capitalism, by no means all the rising bourgeoisie were nonconformist. The other new university of these years, Durham (1832), was anglican, as was Queen's College at Birmingham (1843), which as a later component of the University of Birmingham has as good a claim as Owens to pioneering status. In fact religion was a major source of cultural division in England, and tended to dominate debate on university questions. Anglicans refused to abandon the view that religious and secular education were inseparable, and that universities should be moral and religious as well as intellectual communities. Behind the stubborn defence of the privileges of Oxford and Cambridge lay the persisting ideal of a national élite with common values and experiences, which secularization would destroy.

The most striking feature of the new foundations was their limited success. Durham struggled to survive, and Owens College found no immediate imitators in other cities. The colleges found a niche in teaching new subjects like modern languages, science and economics, but attempts to set up general degree curricula found few takers. An Oxbridge degree had well-understood social advantages, but otherwise formal graduation had little career value, and university education remained ill-defined and not clearly distinguished from secondary schooling. Roman catholics, for example, satisfied their need for higher education through classes attached to secondary schools, and a catholic university founded in London in 1875 collapsed after a few years [79]. Even at Oxford, numbers were stagnant until the 1860s [142].

This weakness of demand contrasted with the economic dynamism of an industrializing Britain, suggesting that for most of the entrepreneurial class, industrialists or merchants, university education was simply irrelevant. In principle, there should have been more demand for professional training, as professional status came to depend on formal qualifications and examinations. But even here there were problems. Medicine led the way: medical schools were founded in London and leading provincial cities in the 1820s and 1830s, and the Act of 1858 which set up a medical register also created a unified system of medical education. Universities and degrees played an important part in this, but only alongside the royal colleges and other qualifying bodies. Other professions like law and engineering, while taking steps to raise their professional status, resisted moves towards academic exclusivism. Most of the new colleges set up courses in these subjects, but had to contend with a strong British prejudice in favour of learning through personal experience and apprenticeship to established practitioners [Engel in 63]. It was only in the 1850s that examinations began to multiply, and that pressure intensified on parents to invest in education to secure their sons' future [107].

That pressure was felt first in the schools. The deficiencies of secondary education had been another source of weakness for the new colleges. Oxford and Cambridge could draw on the ancient public schools, which kept boys until 18 and took classics to a high level. But the ancient network of grammar schools, teaching the classics to local boys and connected with the universities by scholarships, had for various reasons fallen into decay. The middle class instead used private schools, most of which concentrated on commercial and practical subjects, ending at 15 or 16. In London, both UCL and King's founded their own schools to act as feeders, but for the most part the new colleges had to take their students young and start at an elementary level; often students simply used them as staging-posts towards Oxford or Cambridge.

The best documented development in English secondary education is the reform and expansion of the public schools, following Thomas Arnold's work at Rugby. The growing middle class found the reformed schools to their taste, many new ones were funded, and the new model triumphed over possible alternatives. The grammar schools were revived after legislation in 1869, but this was too late to challenge the position of the public schools, and a true system of state secondary education had to await legislation in 1902. Public schools, as boarding institutions, were relatively expensive, but they offered a solid education to the professional and business élite, and pointed them naturally towards Oxford and Cambridge, whose links with the public schools became the foundation of their late Victorian prosperity. Thus although the middle classes did succeed in founding alternative university institutions, in secondary education there was a compromise which adapted the institutions of the old élite to new needs. Once the serious reform of Oxford and Cambridge began, the same compromise could be worked out there, and their opening to a new clientele satisfied a large part of the demand for higher education. Whether this represented a takeover of the old institutions by the middle class, or a takeover of the middle class by the old élite, is a question to which we shall return.

The reform of the old universities, accelerated by state intervention after 1850, has stimulated much scholarship. Interest has switched from the traditional constitutional and religious aspects [147] to the reform of the curriculum and the 'revolution of the dons' which produced a secular, professionalized teaching body [47; 139; 116; 23; 58; 40; 51]. Reform retained the college system, with teaching through tutorial methods rather than professorial lectures, but also remodelled the curriculum to admit modern subjects like history and science. Recent work has stressed that there were many changes even before 1850; but these had concentrated on developing a rigorous examination system, which encouraged the best students to compete for honours. This was perhaps originally designed as a means of social discipline, or to strengthen the aristocratic élite to meet the challenges of a revolutionary age [Rothblatt in 142; Stone in 98], but it soon became especially attractive to students with professional advantages in mind [22]. Here were the origins of the specialized degree, with classified honours, which remains characteristic of the British system. And with the reshaping of the ideal of 'liberal' education, university examinations assumed a new role as the guarantee of professional status.

The nineteenth century saw a notable debate (well covered by historians) on liberal education and on the most appropriate education for the social élite in a newly scientific and industrial world [123; 117; 44; Lyons in 98]. At first Oxbridge intellectuals responded to utilitarian attacks by expounding the unique virtues of classics or mathematics in forming the mind and character, a tradition given its finest expression in J. H. Newman's lectures of the 1850s which became *The Idea of a University*. Others in the 1860s and 1870s like John Stuart Mill, Lyon Playfair or Thomas Huxley, put forward a more comprehensive ideal in which science would take its rightful place. The most influential figure – or at least, the one generally regarded as symbolic – was Matthew Arnold, whose *Culture and Anarchy* (1869), though not directly concerned with universities, popularized the notion of general culture. For Arnold culture was chiefly literary, but one outcome of this debate was to detach the idea of liberal education from its previous association with the classics; now it could be embodied by any subject if taught in a 'liberal' way. This fitted in well with the specialized, single-subject degree and the research ideal, but it also encouraged a bias against the purely vocational.

The Arnoldian ideal was part of a characteristically Victorian complex which tied together liberal education, the concept of the 'gentleman', the public schools, the examination system, the professional and public service ethos, and preference for 'all-rounders' over specialists. A classic example was the competitive civil service examination, first suggested in the Northcote-Trevelyan report of 1853, and applied to most of the senior civil service in 1871. This was both a form of professionalization, substituting impartial selection methods for personal patronage, and a move towards meritocracy. But since the examinations were based on those of the universities, the effect was to open the civil service to the middle class, using liberal education as a social filter and a guarantee of gentlemanly character, rather than drawing talent from all social classes. At Oxford, Balliol College under Benjamin Jowett became renowned for producing an academic élite imbued with the ethic of public service. But although Jowett and others wished to widen the university's social base, this aspect of reform had limited success.

In universities as in public schools, the liberal ideal stressed the moral side of education, for which the socializing experience of residence was thought indispensable. Universities were to be communities, where the intangible benefits of character formation and the personal influence of teachers were as important as the lecture-room [117]. This pastoral concept of the university was not unchallenged – in 1858 London University threw its degrees open to any individual, regardless of institutional affiliation, thus defining university education simply as the mastery of a body of knowledge – but over the years it has profoundly marked the British tradition of higher education.

The university reforms can be interpreted as a conservative social strategy, against a background of growing democracy (the vote was extended to working men in 1867), state-supported popular education, and the decline of religion as an integrating force. The aim was to strengthen the influence of the educated classes, to form a 'clerisy' giving the nation intellectual and spiritual leadership. Once free from their exclusive connexion with anglicanism (the tests for students had been abolished in the 1850s), the universities were restored to a central position in national life, able to absorb and civilize the new bourgeoisie and blend it into a single élite [106; 58; 73; Rothblatt in 63]. Even if this programme was not fully achieved, it is especially significant for university history that the revival of the old universities took place before the expansion of the new ones really began, making it difficult for the latter to challenge their values, and attracting away the richer provincial élites.

Owens College was virtually refounded in 1870–1, and by 1881 it had been joined by university colleges (full university status often came considerably later) at Newcastle, Leeds, Sheffield, Birmingham, Liverpool, Nottingham and Bristol. Later additions, in less industrial towns, were Southampton, Reading and Exeter. Sometimes there were gifts or legacies from wealthy individuals, but in all cases it was local business and professional men who took the initiative and superintended development. Colleges often started with a strong practical emphasis related to local industry, but there were also roots in the long-established medical schools and in the 'extension' lectures by which the older universities, especially Cambridge, had sought to take liberal education to the provinces. By the 1900s the 'civic' or 'redbrick' colleges were offering a wide range of subjects, and more of their students were taking full courses leading to degrees – in the early years, there had been much work at a lower level, and much part-time study in evening classes. This standardization of the pattern was partly to meet the conditions laid down by the state for awarding grants or the prized royal charters which gave degree-granting powers.

The state played a more active role in university development than is often recognized. Annual grants to university colleges began in 1889, and legislation of the same period on technical education gave elected local authorities an active role. Sometimes their funds went into direct support of the local college – Nottingham was founded and directly controlled by the city council; more often, they built up technical colleges which had some work of degree standard, and which entered into cooperative relationships with the university – at Manchester, for example, the municipal technical college became its Faculty of Technology. By

1914 colleges on the grant list got about a third of their income from the state, and another 15 per cent from local authorities.

Universities also profited from the organization of state secondary education after 1902. New or reorganized grammar schools were strongly oriented towards academic subjects and university entrance; senior pupils worked for university 'matriculation' examinations (coordinated from 1917 as the School Certificate), and Oxbridge scholarships were their blue riband. The policies of Robert Morant (the civil servant at the head of the Board of Education) have been much criticized for stifling practical alternatives and relegating technology to an inferior role, but they reflected the view (also found in the contemporary adult education movement) that extending opportunity to the working class meant a right to share in liberal education of the highest form. From 1907 the introduction of 'free places' ensured that scholarship children from elementary schools sat in the grammar schools alongside middle-class children whose parents paid fees. But it was significant for the future, and a point which distinguished Britain from other countries, that the machinery of state-sponsored opportunity was developed within a second-rank system, rather than by opening up the public schools which gave direct access to the élite.

Training graduate teachers for secondary schools became a large part of the work of arts and science faculties. Universities also acquired a share in training elementary teachers. Training colleges, mostly run by the churches, went back to the early nineteenth century, and were always an important channel of social mobility. From 1890 universities were allowed to set up their own 'day training colleges', which brought an influx of working-class students financed by the state. Later developments allowed them to graduate before starting the professional part of the course.

Schoolteaching was the main occupation chosen by women students, whose admission to universities was another feature of the period after 1870. Academic secondary schools for girls, with the same curriculum as for boys, began to develop in the 1850s [26]. The universities helped by opening their 'local' examinations for school-leavers to girls, and by the late 1860s many towns had lectures of university level for women. The pressure for admission to proper university study was reinforced by the campaign for women's medical education, and achieved success in the 1870s.

The new university colleges were open to women from the start, and London University degrees from 1878. At Oxford and Cambridge, the collegiate system made it relatively easy to found women's colleges, though numbers were small and equal academic status was denied for many years. In London, UCL opened to women on equal terms, but there were also women's colleges, including 'King's College for Women' on a separate site from the original college. By 1900, when girls' secondary schools were everywhere a normal part of middle-class life, women university students had also consolidated their position, though their numbers were limited by the scarcity of outlets. Training in social work and in domestic subjects (a speciality of King's College for Women) were curricular innovations which sought to respond to women's needs.

Why had the state taken a new interest in universities? One reason was growing international economic and great-power competition, especially from Germany; education was identified as a field where Britain was falling behind. This mood intensified after the Boer war of 1899–1902, and was expressed in the 'national efficiency' movement, which looked to vigorous state action to exploit Britain's human resources. This included the more efficient discovery and selection of merit, and the free places of 1907 were part of a deliberate Liberal policy of extending educational opportunity. Sanderson has emphasized that 'this brief period of the 1900s was of profound significance in the development of access to education' [125, 25].

According to Sidney Webb, 'nothing is more calculated to promote National Efficiency, than a large policy of Government aid to the highest technical colleges and universities' [cited in 48, 182]. Sidney and Beatrice Webb founded the London School of Economics in 1895 to apply scientific principles to business and public administration, and they were not the only political figures active on the educational scene. Others were Joseph Chamberlain, patron of Birmingham University, and Richard Haldane, who was involved in many enterprises, including a major reorganization of London University in 1898, and the foundation of Imperial College London (1907), which amalgamated several existing science colleges and was Britain's answer to the German 'technical high schools' [19].

Between 1870 and 1914, and especially after 1889, English universities not only expanded, but came to form a system with common ideals and standards, to which other British universities were increasingly assimilated. There were various pressures behind this: the common requirements of the professions and public services, the prestige of the internationally-accepted research ideal, the development of an academic profession which circulated freely throughout the system [54]. But not least there was the Oxbridge model, and it is widely accepted that the original dynamism and distinctiveness of the civic universities gave way to imitation – according to Jarausch, they 'altered their entire mission from higher technical training towards the traditional university function' [63, *19*].

The fullest account of this, within the framework of 'systematization', is by Roy Lowe. He argues that the system became hierarchical, with Oxford, Cambridge and London at the top, the civic universities second, and (looking at higher education as a whole) technical and teacher training colleges as a third layer. By shedding their part-time and non-degree work, the civics were as anxious to distinguish themselves from the layer below as they were to adopt the university model. The outcome was that they gave the same sort of education as the élite universities, but with less prestige and for a local rather than a national clientele. Thus there emerged 'an educational system which by the time of the First World War had become segmented at various levels, the better to serve the needs of a differentiated society'. While Oxbridge remained aloof and protected from change, at the second level there was 'a reversion from the modernism of the late nineteenth century towards a more prestigious "humane" education' [Lowe in 92, *177*; cf. Halsey in 53; 54; 105; Lowe and Rothblatt in 63]. The common tendency of institutions founded for practical or specialist purposes to abandon them for activities of higher prestige has been called the 'generalist shift' by Ringer, 'academic drift' by others.

This view of Oxbridge dominance is so familiar as hardly to need stressing. British cultural history is often told in terms of university cliques and influences [15], and since so many of the political, literary and artistic élite were educated at Oxford or Cambridge, they figure in countless memoirs, biographies and

Table 1.1 *Student numbers, 1861–1901*

|  | 1861 | 1871 | 1881 | 1891 | 1901 |
|---|---|---|---|---|---|
| *Oxford and Cambridge* | | | | | |
| No. | 2400 | 3690 | 4710 | 5100 | 5880 |
| per cent increase | | 54 | 28 | 8 | 15 |
| *Other English* | | | | | |
| No. | 985 | 1840 | 5963 | 10,913 | 11,959 |
| per cent increase | | 87 | 224 | 83 | 10 |
| *England* | | | | | |
| No. | 3385 | 5530 | 10,673 | 16,013 | 17,839 |
| Per 1000 population | 0.2 | 0.2 | 0.4 | 0.6 | 0.5 |
| *Scotland* | | | | | |
| No. | 3399 | 3984 | 6595 | 6604 | 6254 |
| per cent increase | | 17 | 66 | 0 | − 19 |
| Per 1000 population | 1.1 | 1.2 | 1.8 | 1.6 | 1.4 |

*Sources:* [63, 45; 9, 467].

novels – including novels of university life which, so argues Ian Carter [29], have further reinforced the image of the ancient universities and endorsed their conservative values. In other universities, professors recruited from Oxbridge brought their ideals and prejudices with them, and subjects like classics or history, developed as part of the education of a governing class [132; 133; 136; 137; 138], were taught in the same way to prospective schoolteachers. Civic universities began to develop halls of residence and tutorial systems, university histories celebrated the triumphant march to chartered status, and student life took on new corporate forms inspired by the collegiate ideal [11]. Yet the capitulation to Oxbridge values can be exaggerated, and there are counter-arguments which will be examined in Chapter 3.

By 1900, Oxbridge accounted for only a third of English students. This is shown in Table 1.1, which compares statistics compiled by Lowe for England (many of them estimates) with those for Scotland. The table shows the percentage increase in each decade, and the number of students per 1000 total population, a crude but useful means of comparison. Once population growth is allowed for there was little real expansion in Scotland, which already had some 2850 students in 1800 (1.8 per 1000), at a

Table 1.2 *Student numbers, 1900–1938*

|  | 1900 | 1910 | 1920 | 1930 | 1938 |
|---|---|---|---|---|---|
| *England* | | | | | |
| No. | 13,845 | 19,617 | 33,868 | 33,808 | 37,189 |
| per cent women | 15 | 18 | 23 | 25 | 22 |
| *Wales* | | | | | |
| No. | 1253 | 1375 | 2838 | 2868 | 2779 |
| per cent women | 38 | 35 | 28 | 33 | 27 |
| *Scotland* | | | | | |
| No. | 5151 | 6736 | 11,746 | 11,150 | 10,034 |
| per cent women | 14 | 24 | 26 | 32 | 27 |
| *Great Britain* | | | | | |
| No. | 20,249 | 27,728 | 48,452 | 47,826 | 50,002 |
| per cent women | 16 | 20 | 24 | 27 | 23 |

*Source:* University Grants Committee reports.

time when Oxford and Cambridge together had about 1150. Within the existing assumptions about the social function of university education, Scotland reached the limits of expansion early and could not go beyond them; the figures thus cast doubt on the notion of 'seismic' growth resulting from industrialization. In England, there was plenty of leeway to catch up, but once this happened the pace fell off. The most dynamic decade in both countries was the 1870s, which suggests that this was the period when graduation became accepted as a standard professional aspiration.

Table 1.2 shows student numbers after 1900. There was significant growth before the First World War, and a leap in numbers after it. Enrolments remained on the new plateau, but then stagnated or declined. The 1930s were a difficult decade for universities, especially since the depression and the cuts in public expenditure after 1931 made schoolteaching an unattractive career. This particularly affected the recruitment of women: the percentage of women students reached a peak at the end of the 1920s, but then declined, and remained stuck at 23–24 per cent until the 1960s. For recent periods, it is also possible to calculate the 'age participation ratio' (APR), the proportion of the age-group which attended university. This was about 0.8 per cent for Great

Britain in the 1900s (and thus perhaps 1.5 per cent in Scotland), 1.5 per cent in 1924, and 1.7 per cent in 1938 (1.5 per cent in England and Wales, 3.1 per cent in Scotland). If other forms of higher education were included, the 1938 figure would be 2.7 per cent, but university education remained very much a minority experience [109, *16*; 105, *229–30*].

The two world wars are usually seen as catalysts for social change, but their effects on higher education were not the same. The First World War followed a period of active expansion, and reconstruction plans were based on the pre-war policies of the Liberal government [128]. The dynamism of the pre-war period was carried over into the 1920s, but then petered out. In 1939, by contrast, higher education was stagnant: the war itself seems to have created a new mood of social expectation, and post-war policies led into a continually rising curve of growth.

The 1918 Education Act (like that of 1944) was not directly concerned with universities, but the war was followed by significant changes. In 1919 the University Grants Committee (UGC) was created to unify administration of grants in England, Wales and Scotland, and introduced an element of central planning; Oxford and Cambridge were now brought into the grant system. New university colleges were founded at Leicester and Hull. Local authority scholarships multiplied, and a limited number of national state scholarships was introduced. Subjects like modern languages, engineering, science and commerce expanded, and the idea of universities leading to business careers gained ground. But their fundamental association with the professions remained, and if there was a new influx of scholarship students it hardly changed the social atmosphere. Oxford and Cambridge retained their upper-class image and their bond with the public schools. In retrospect, it may seem that investment in higher education, especially in science and technology, would have prepared Britain for recovery from the depression. But neither contemporary governments nor the cautious-minded UGC thought in such terms [16].

The experience of the Second World War, however, gave new prestige to science and planning, and reconstruction plans accepted that university numbers would have to expand by at least 50 per cent. There was also a new emphasis on equality of opportunity, as part of the post-war 'welfare state' settlement which aimed to break down class divisions and extend the social rights of citizenship. The English Act of 1944 abolished fees in secondary schools (this had been done in Scotland in 1918), and introduced 'secondary education for all'. But this was to follow the 'tripartite' organization of grammar, technical and modern schools, and only the grammar schools, recruited selectively through the '11+' examination and taking about a fifth of the age-group, led to universities. Nevertheless, systematic selection replaced the arbitrary scholarship 'ladder', and the expansion of qualified school-leavers stimulated by this reform created a wholly new demand for higher education.

Stress on technology was also characteristic of the post-war years, though opinion was divided on whether to put resources into universities or into building up selected technical colleges. Ten of the latter were eventually designated as Colleges of Advanced Technology (CATs), and in the 1960s these were given full university status, along with two Scottish equivalents. But there were also new foundations devoted to the liberal ideal. North Staffordshire (later Keele) was an experimental university founded in 1949, and in the 1950s plans were laid for a series of 'green field' sites. Sussex opened first in 1961, and was followed by York, East Anglia, Essex, Lancaster, Kent and Warwick. These residential (in some cases collegiate) universities were a striking triumph of the pastoral ideal. They would hardly have been possible without another significant development, the introduction of uniform, 'mandatory' student grants in 1962, following the Anderson report. Any school-leaver accepted for a place now had a right to have living expenses away from home paid as well as fees. This broke the link between civic universities and their localities, and with the creation of a unified admissions procedure turned British universities for the first time into a single system with national recruitment.

All this preceded the Robbins report (1963), which 'could do little more than legitimise what by then had become inevitable' [77, *172*]. Its significance lay partly in its proclamation of the 'Robbins principle' ('courses of higher education should be available for all those who are qualified by ability and attainment to pursue them and who wish to do so' [109, *8*]), partly in its statistical work, which seemed to make the case for expansion irrefutable, and partly in looking at 'higher education' as a whole. The report aroused a remarkable degree of political support, and provides a prime example of the 'post-war consensus' on social reform (which did not extend to secondary education, where the selective grammar schools were now coming under attack). Successive governments, believing that higher education was a key to economic growth, found resources to meet the targets for expansion.

But Robbins's administrative proposals, for a unitary structure with universities in a coordinating role, found less favour. Instead the 1964 Labour government's 'binary' policy divided higher education between a university sector under the UGC and a 'public' sector consisting mainly of local authority colleges. There were no more new universities in England (though Scotland acquired one at Stirling), apart from the Open University, teaching adults by distance learning. Nevertheless, the Robbins period left Great Britain with over 50 universities – over 70 if the colleges of London University were counted separately. Within the public sector, there were many amalgamations, and colleges of education (as training colleges had been renamed) lost their specialized character. In England and Wales, some thirty larger colleges were developed as 'polytechnics'; in Scotland, the binary system took a different form, with the leading colleges under the direct control of the Scottish Education Department. In the 1990s, however, the dual structure in place since the 1960s was scheduled to disappear, with polytechnics gaining university status, and separate 'funding councils', covering the whole of higher education, for England, Wales and Scotland. All these arrangements (like most of the statistics below) excluded Northern Ireland, which had never come directly under the UGC, or under the scrutiny of Robbins; developments there followed similar lines, but the binary line broke down sooner when the polytechnic at Belfast was merged with the New University of Ulster founded at Coleraine in the 1960s.

In 1962 the Robbins committee found 216,000 full-time students in higher education in Great Britain: 118,000 in universities, 55,000 in teacher training, 43,000 in 'advanced further education' (technical colleges). Its projection of 558,000 places in 1980 was not quite met – there were to be 301,000 in universities and

223,000 in the public sector [56, *270, 275*]. But the public sector then expanded more rapidly, and by 1990 there were about 650,000 full-time students in the United Kingdom, 340,000 in universities, 310,000 in colleges; if part-time and Open University students were included, the total was nearly a million. The result of this expansion was that the university APR, still only 3.4 per cent in 1955 and 4 per cent in 1962, rose to about 8 per cent by the mid-1980s, when for higher education as a whole it was 14 per cent [56, *270*; 141, *278*].

Numerical expansion was accompanied by formal equalization of standards, as three or four year degrees replaced the diplomas or certificates to which much college work had formerly led. But in one respect the Robbins projections were not met: the demand for humanities and social science subjects proved stronger than for science and technology, where places fell well short of the targets. As Carswell has argued [28], this was partly because there was no corresponding reform of schools, partly because women accounted for a significant part of the Robbins expansion. In 1958, only 24 per cent of university students were women, but the proportion rose to 28 per cent in 1968, 38 per cent in 1980, and 40 per cent in 1984 [141, *279*]. By 1989 it was 44 per cent – still lower than in many comparable countries. The rise was due predominantly to wider changes in society, especially the increasing career opportunities for women in business and the professions; but there were also controlling factors within education itself, as Cunningham [33] has shown for Scotland, where a less segmented school system was one reason for consistently higher women's participation rates.

What was the historical significance of the post-war expansion? While scholarly inquiry has begun to tackle the inter-war period [130], for the years since 1945 it remains at the stage of provisional synthesis [77; 141]. Otherwise we are dependent on contemporary analyses, or the recollections and reflections of participants. The commonest theme has been the survival of the liberal ideal despite the move towards a mass system. The traditional model was endorsed by Robbins, and the academic ethos reigned supreme [14; 15; 127; 28]. The binary system protected the status of the universities, and can be seen as a further example of 'segmentation' reflecting social inequalities [77]. While in principle all higher education enjoyed parity of esteem, the diversion of new students into cheaper and less prestigious institutions allowed the universities, old and new, to retain such élite features as residence and the single-subject degree. The latter was indeed encouraged by the specialized Advanced Level examination introduced in the 1950s (though not in Scotland) to replace the broader-based School Certificate, and by a grant system which favoured the full-time student coming straight from school. Expansion thus changed the character of the universities less than the conservative authors of the educational 'Black Papers' in the early 1970s feared, or than some reformers hoped. Polytechnics and colleges had a different ethos which stressed vocational subjects, retained links with the local community, and welcomed part-time students. But even they (like the CATs before them) were tempted by 'academic drift' to expand into arts and pure science.

British development seemed to diverge in this period from that in other countries. In the 1900s or the 1930s, participation rates were not out of line with comparable countries, but in the 1950s Britain began to lag noticeably behind, and this was one of the arguments for expansion used by Robbins [125]. By the 1980s, while British participation rates rose towards 20 per cent for all higher education, the western European norm was becoming 30–40 per cent, and it was higher still in America or Japan. Other European countries generally retained open university entry for all who passed the qualifying school examinations, so that the democratization of secondary schooling brought huge increases, with consequent problems of overcrowding, impersonal teaching and high drop-out rates. But Britain chose a more expensive form of growth, with residential universities, mandatory grants, and intensive teaching supported by high staff-student ratio. This tied state funding to specific student numbers, and inhibited the transition to a true mass system. By the 1970s, strains were appearing as the social pressures for university expansion continued but governments became less willing to provide the resources. The 1980s saw moves to replace grants with loans and attract private funding by making universities more responsive to market forces.

It is difficult to say whether alternative policies were seriously considered in the 1960s. It seems more likely that the traditional university model was simply taken for granted, as one more example of the London-Oxbridge axis in British life [129]. The ideals of the redbricks or the technical colleges failed to impose themselves on the debate, and in practical terms open entry would not have been compatible with the special position of Oxbridge and its collegiate system. Thus the weight of the past determined the direction of progress, and for the same reason it seems unlikely that the abolition of the binary division will remove the hierarchy of prestige and function which British higher education displays. Every country, indeed, has such hierarchies; but it is history which dictates the form they take.

## 2

# Nations and cultures

Generalization about British universities has not always taken account of the multi-national character of the British state. Yet universities have been central in forming the élites of its component nations and promoting or maintaining their distinctive cultures. Both Scotland and Ireland, as historic nations, had their own landed and professional élites, who staffed the local administrative and judicial institutions, and university cities like Edinburgh, Glasgow or Dublin had an independent cultural life. Wales had no university in 1800, but was to acquire one aspiring to a similar national role. The relationship of these universities to élite formation within the British state, and in the Irish case within the nation itself, was never simple. Oxford and Cambridge, like the English public schools, always appealed to the aristocracy and the wealthiest of the middle classes, and after their reform they attracted Scottish, Welsh and (protestant) Irish families in significant numbers. To this extent there was a single British élite. But most of the local middle classes felt a dual allegiance: while identifying politically with Britain, and having no desire for separation, they valued their local cultural identity and supported the schools and universities on their doorstep. Thus the latter were never so overshadowed by Oxford and Cambridge as the new English universities, and were a counterweight to metropolitan influence when the demand for university education expanded. Universities like Aberdeen, Glasgow or Belfast established a dominance in training the professional and business leaders of their regions never quite achieved by the English civics. There was not the same pressure for uniformity as in countries like France, where the formation of a homogeneous élite was seen as essential to the unity of a modern nation-state, or Germany, where the universities were focuses of national identity before the central state itself was formed.

The most complex case was Ireland, where the 'university question' reflected the clash of religions and cultures and the failure to form a common Irish nationality. The catholic élite rejected a dual allegiance in favour of a purely national one, and created its own university, which cultivated a separate cultural identity pointing forward to political partition and secession. As very often happened in the history of nationalism, universities and the university-formed intelligentsia were the creators of national myths and ideologies. The same was true of Wales, though its nationalism remained cultural and not political. In Scotland, the universities' links with the Presbyterian church gave them a traditional cultural character very different from anglican Oxbridge, but when these links weakened in the nineteenth century it was not clear what would replace them, and the relationship of Scottish universities to national identity has proved contentious: they often seemed uninterested in national literary and cultural movements, and were accused of being 'anglicized'.

Scotland had the strongest university system of the three 'peripheral' nations. Having embarked early on industrialization, it was the only one to have a large urban bourgeoisie. With a tenth of England's populaton, it had four university centres, at Aberdeen, Edinburgh, Glasgow, and St Andrews. The universities had reached a peak of fame during the Enlightenment, when Oxford and Cambridge languished, and lived on this intellectual capital well into the nineteenth century. The long-established cultural and political interchange with England gave the Scottish universities a strong influence on metropolitan intellectual, literary and scientific life, and they served as models for foundations like UCL [108].

The reasons for their success were the obverse of the reasons why Oxford and Cambridge stagnated. While providing a liberal education for the leisured classes, the Scottish universities did not neglect professional training. The faculties of law and divinity served the areas of Scottish life which had retained their autonomy since the union, while the very successful medical schools exported graduates to the rest of the British Isles. The universities benefited from the religious homogeneity of presbyterian Scotland, and had no religious tests for students. Situated in large towns (apart from St Andrews), they were easily accessible to part-time students, who were numerous, and their curriculum, based on professorial lectures, could be taken selectively and flexibly – until the 1880s, the majority of students did not formally graduate. The universities' urban character also made them socially diverse. Fees were relatively low, there was no residential requirement, the university ethos stressed frugality and hard work rather than aristocratic dissipation, and bursaries for poorer students were widely available. Not least, Scotland had a more accessible school system than England. Scottish 'burgh schools' served the urban middle classes efficiently, and in the countryside there was a national system of parish schools from which, because it was the custom to appoint as schoolmasters university men who could teach Latin, students could enter university directly. This was commonly at 15 or 16, and the university curriculum began at a correspondingly elementary level. This complex of arrangements gave the universities a 'popular character' much celebrated by patriots.

Precocious development meant less pressure for change in Scotland and less expansion of student numbers. But there were various organizational defects which attracted state intervention, leading to royal commissions in 1826 and 1876 and important legislation in 1858 and 1889. This reform movement has attracted historians, and controversy has been especially lively in the wake of G. E. Davie's book *The Democratic Intellect* [34], the argument of which he has recently extended to the 1920s and 1930s [35]. Davie sees 'anglicization' as the key to the reform process, and deplores the way in which the Scottish élite lost its national integrity through the adoption of the English model, particularly after 1889, when specialized honours degrees began to replace the distinctively Scottish broad curriculum based on philosophy. Davie sees a link between this philosophical approach and the democratic sympathies of the national intellectual leadership which it shaped. Against Davie, it has been argued that reform was inspired by adaptation to social changes common to England and Scotland, and by the career demands of the Scottish middle classes. Professionalization, civil service examinations and the proliferation of opportunities in the British empire were factors common to all parts of Britain, and demanded more uniform curricula. Thus a nationalist interpretation in terms of rival anglicizing and patriotic parties distorts and simplifies a complex set of controversies [7]. Davie may also oversimplify the contrast between Scottish general and English specialized curricula, for in the nineteenth century multi-subject curricula were common, notably in the London BA and in Ireland; the teaching of philosophy was hardly a Scottish monopoly, and the Oxbridge ideal was itself one of general humane education [150]. In each country, the research ideal and the development of disciplines was the force behind specialization.

Davie's thesis has had an influence well outside academic circles, touching a chord during the nationalist revivals which have characterised Scottish politics since the 1960s, and appealing to those who feel the need to reconstitute an independent Scottish intelligentsia. It reinforced the egalitarian 'myth' of Scottish education which has always had a strong popular appeal, and took on new significance with the possibility of political devolution returning control of the universities to Scottish hands. These issues, along with such features as the consistently higher APR in Scotland, have stimulated interest among historians and sociologists in the roots of the Scottish tradition [82; 84; 8; 30]. The sentimental power of the myth, it has been argued, has sometimes obscured the real inequalities within Scotland. For Scottish universities, whatever romantic feeling might cling to the 'lad of parts' who arrived from a poor home or a remote village to study in a garret, never neglected their chief task of serving the professional and business classes.

Nevertheless, research shows that the lad of parts did exist. It was possible for the sons of small farmers, shopkeepers or artisans to reach the university and become ministers or school-masters – though the opportunities for the children of factory workers, miners or rural labourers were far more restricted. There is plenty of evidence for this pattern of recruitment in the 1860s, when 20 per cent or more of students could be considered 'working class' [7], and W. M. Mathew's work [86] shows it already established at Glasgow by the 1830s. Thus Scotland forms an acknowledged exception to Kaelble's theory on the chronology of educational opportunity [69].

Innovations in Scotland after 1889 included the distinction between four-year honours degrees and three-year 'ordinary' ones, the admission of women (rather late) in 1892, and the active development of secondary education by the state. In 1892 the universities introduced a compulsory entrance examination, which corresponded to the national Leaving Certificate for schools, and the average age of entry rose to 18. The traditional route from parish school to university was replaced by a secondary school ladder. But the result was extension rather than decline of opportunity. In the 1900s, there were more working and lower middle class students than in the 1860s, and the proportion had not changed significantly by the 1930s, or indeed the 1960s [7; 11; 80; see also Table 5.2]. In their dual role of renewing the local élite and injecting a Scottish element into the national one, the Scottish universities could draw on a wide social base.

The same came to be true of the University of Wales. Although St David's College Lampeter was founded in 1827 to train anglican clergyman, and acquired degree-granting powers, the Welsh university movement was associated with the nonconformist, Welsh-speaking culture of the chapels. Demand for cheap, non-denominational colleges coincided with industrialization and the growth of a middle class in search of professional training. The first college was founded at Aberystwyth in 1872, with the aid of collections in workplaces and chapels ('the pennies of the poor') [39]. The movement was given official sanction by the Aberdare report (1881), followed by a state grant and the foundation of colleges at Cardiff and Bangor. The University of Wales was set up in 1893 as a federal examining university, and a fourth college at Swansea was opened in 1920. The new colleges owed much to the expanding school system, especially after 1889, when legislation introduced 'intermediate' schools which brought secondary education to country towns and industrial valleys, achieving remarkably high rates of penetration. Their curriculum stressed academic subjects, and critics complained that they turned out too many schoolteachers and clerks, and not enough productive workers. But as in Scotland, popular opinion valued social mobility and insisted that the working class should not be cut off from Latin, which opened the door to the professions and the universities. In both countries, schoolteaching became the great object of ambition for scholars from poor backgrounds, and, along with training for the ministry, provided the colleges with much of their custom.

The university rapidly established a special place in Welsh life, and education was seen as a symbol of national identity, cultural achievement and popular emancipation. The colleges made a vital contribution to the cultural revival of Wales, and produced a nationally-minded, Welsh-speaking intelligentsia, active in politics and literature as well as in the educational world; nowhere more than in Wales did educationists play such a prominent part in public life. By 1914 Wales had its own democratic myth of a 'university of the people', turning out poets, pastors and professors with their roots in the soil [91]. The myth was vindicated by the facts, for the available statistics – including a useful series for Lampeter [101] – show that while the majority of students were the children of ministers, doctors, farmers or small businessmen, the proportion of working-class students, including miners and other manual workers, was even higher than in Scotland – a third or more by 1914 [149, *289*; 12]. This ratio was to be maintained, as was the high proportion of women students, an outcome of the interest in teaching careers.

The cultural role of the university continued between the wars, but later sharply diminished with the decline of the language and the collapse of nonconformist chapel culture. The federal university survived, eventually absorbing Lampeter, and periodic attempts by individual colleges to break away were resisted in the name of nationalism. Nationalist grievances were also expressed in the demand for more Welsh-language teaching and Welsh-speaking halls of residence. But despite these campaigns, and in contrast with Scotland, by the 1990s less than a third of the students were Welsh. Welsh students preferred to go to England, and unlike Scottish ones they were not restrained by different school-leaving qualifications. It thus seems doubtful how much national character the university retains, and the study of university history has not had the same political resonance as in Scotland.

In Ireland, the university question was never without political implications. In 1800 there was only one university, Trinity College Dublin (TCD), which served the protestant landed and professional class. It resembled the Scottish universities in giving a sound professional training, but lacked their democratic aspect. It was, above all, strongly anglican in character, even though tests had been abolished for students in 1794. Thus TCD satisfied neither the catholic majority, nor the presbyterians of the north; but the latter, unlike the other denominations, were prepared to accept mixed or non-denominational colleges rather than ones controlled by themselves. Traditionally Ulster looked to Scotland to train its ministers and doctors, but local needs expanded with the rise of Belfast as an industrial city. The Belfast Academical Institution of 1814 has a good claim to be the first new 'university' of the nineteenth century, for although it combined secondary and higher education, it acquired faculties of theology and medicine as well as arts, and received a state subsidy.

Its higher work was transferred in 1849 to Queen's College Belfast (QCB), one of three non-denominational colleges promoted by the state (the others were at Cork and Galway); the Queen's University to award degrees to their students followed in 1850. The British government hoped that these colleges, directed at the middle classes, would form an Irish élite rising above party and religion, and loyal to the British connexion; in particular, it was hoped to detach the catholic laity from supposed clerical domination. But this plan failed from the start. It was condemned by the Church, hostile on principle to mixed education and the separation of religious and secular instruction. The logical consequence was the foundation of a Catholic University at Dublin, opened in 1854 with Newman as rector – his *Idea of a University* lectures were originally given in preparation for this. The Catholic University was not very successful, and was moribund when taken over by the Jesuits in 1883, after which it revived as University College Dublin (UCD).

Irish higher education suffered from difficulties familiar in England – the underdevelopment of secondary schools, especially for catholics, and limited demand for anything but vocational education; the medical school was the most successful part of the Catholic University, as of the Queen's Colleges. Although QCB drew from lower social strata than TCD, and from rural Ulster as much as from Belfast [89], nineteenth-century Ireland was unable to develop a 'democratic' university tradition of the Scottish or Welsh type. But such difficulties were compounded by politics and religion. TCD and the Queen's College, endowed or supported by the state, satisfied the demands of anglicans and presbyterians. The catholics claimed similar support, but British governments could not give it, because of the strength of protestant opinion in British politics, and because non-denominationalism had become the orthodox policy for higher education; Ireland was an exception to the secularizing trend seen elsewhere. In the 1860s and 1870s successive attempts to devise a framework acceptable to catholics failed, though the remaining anglican restrictions at TCD were abolished in 1873, and in 1879 the Queen's University was replaced by the Royal University of Ireland, an open examining university like London. This allowed some state money to be channelled to UCD, and gave access to degrees to other institutions like the presbyterian Magee College at Londonderry (1865), and the colleges for women in Belfast and Dublin.

The result was that the different communities had separate systems of higher (as of secondary) education, expressing their distinctive values and emphasizing what divided them. TCD remained the stronghold of the ascendancy and southern unionism [78; 81], and was the subject of a 'ban' by the Vatican. UCD, on the other hand, came to be identified with nationalism and the Gaelic revival, and saw its mission as not just to train a catholic middle class equipped to compete for professional positions, but to embody the catholic definition of Ireland's cultural traditions and to form a new national élite. From the 1880s nationalist MPs consistently supported the catholic case. After a further series of commissions and inquiries in the 1900s, legislation of 1908 accepted these divisions. The Royal University was replaced by a National University of Ireland, which included UCD and the former Queen's Colleges at Cork and Galway. The National University was formally secular, and could thus be supported by the state, but in reality it embodied and satisfied catholic aspirations. TCD remained independent, while in the north QCB became the freestanding Queen's University of Belfast (QUB).

Thus over the years all schemes for a single national university had been frustrated, and 'the university settlement of 1908 . . . was in a profoundly significant sense the prelude to the partition of Ireland in 1921' [88, *109*]. After that date universities in southern Ireland pass outside our scope. QUB came under the control of the new Northern Ireland government, and developed on similar lines to English civic universities. But after 1908, though drawing on a school system strictly segregated by religion, it succeeded in attracting catholic students and acting, in belated justification of the original non-denominational principle, as a point of union for the contending communities of the province.

# 3
# Middle class values

In the pattern of university development suggested in Chapter 1, a modern alternative at first challenged tradition, but later compromised with it, leading to the emergence of a single national system in which élite characteristics prevailed. Many historians see the general course of British social development in similar terms. The entrepreneurial middle class, it is alleged, failed to make its own values dominant, and was assimilated into the traditional élite. W. D. Rubinstein, for example, has argued from his research into the distribution of wealth that in the nineteenth century there were 'two middle classes' – one metropolitan, commercial, and anglican, with close ties to the old landed class, the other provincial, industrial and nonconformist. Contrary to the popular view of the industrial revolution, more wealth was generated from commerce and finance in the south than from industry in the north, so that when these classes merged into a single bourgeoisie in the twentieth century it was the older establishment and its values which prevailed [121]. Rubinstein's suggestion, not fully demonstrated empirically, is that patronage of the public schools and Oxbridge can be associated especially with the 'southern' middle class.

Should we see in the foundation of the civic universities the assertion of a distinctively provincial culture? Of course a simple contrast between 'metropolitan' Oxbridge and the provinces is inadequate, because the London colleges, patronized by business and professional families, stood for values which were modern and scientific without being specifically industrial [119]. Nevertheless, institutional histories of the civic colleges, which usually treat the foundation years very fully, leave little doubt that local élites had a vigorous sense of civic pride; universities, like museums or art galleries, were meant to assert the cultural maturity of the great Victorian cities. A recent study of the early years of Manchester, Leeds and Liverpool emphasizes their consciously middle-class character, and that they stood for the 'independent bourgeois culture' of the north [66, 27]. But Jones also shows the complexity of the motives involved. Although some of the new foundations put a special emphasis on science and technology (like Leeds and Mason College Birmingham), wider professional and occupational needs were never neglected.

Nor can the new colleges be associated exclusively with non-conformism, despite the importance of founders like Owens and Mason, or the group of unitarians who were so prominent in the early years of Liverpool [70]. A study of the educational strategies of local élites in Birmingham and Sheffield shows how rival groups, divided on religious lines, promoted different sets of institutions [135]. More research needs to be done on the local politics of higher education, but it seems clear that in the early nineteenth century religion was a key determinant of cultural identity for middle-class groups within England, as it was between the British nations; and cultural differences faded accordingly as the secularization of the educated classes paved the way to fusion.

In Rubinstein's perspective, the industrial revolution was a revolution which failed, absorbed by the elastic fabric of British society. Other historians have expressed comparable ideas, which break down into three linked but distinct propositions: that the middle classes failed to establish their own cultural dominance, and surrendered to the preindustrial landed class; that there was a major divide within the middle class between the gentrified professional sector and those engaged in industry and commerce; and that British élite values transmitted through education embodied an 'anti-entrepreneurial' culture which had debilitating effects on economic performance.

The first thesis has been most vigorously stated by Marxist historians, notably Perry Anderson, though it contrasts with the more orthodox Marxist view, represented by the earlier work of Brian Simon [131], that the structure of education was dictated by the class interests of triumphant capitalism. For Anderson, the class assimilation promoted by the reformed public schools and universities was actually a triumph for the aristocracy, which was able to retain its position as the leading part of a modernized ruling class [5; 6; cf. Simon in 92; 46]. One result was that instead of generating a radical, dissident intelligentsia as in continental countries, universities expressed the liberal but conformist values of the establishment. This theory about the failure of the British intelligentsia and their attraction to gentlemanly values has become well-established [52; 60], and was indeed pioneered in the 1950s by non-Marxists like Edward Shils [129] and Noel Annan. In his essay on the 'intellectual aristocracy', Annan showed how the academic dynasties of reformed Oxbridge, linked by marriage and kinship, integrated the university world into other parts of the political and public-service élite [13].

Anderson's view of Britain can be fitted into the wider argument of Arno J. Mayer that throughout Europe the power of the landed élite and the 'feudal', pre-industrial and 'pre-bourgeois' order survived until the First World War, with traditional education based on the classics acting as the ideological rampart of the old regime. But however plausible this may be for countries like Germany, its application to Britain relies on a stereotype of Oxbridge and public school dominance, and ignores the growth of science and practical subjects even in those privileged strongholds, the meritocratic examination machinery constructed by the Victorians, and the advanced educational policies of pre-war liberalism. Nevertheless, Mayer's view that élite education 'deflected the sons of the ever apostatizing bourgeoisie from disesteemed industry, trade, and engineering, which were considered unworthy, into honourable careers in the civil and colonial service, the Church, the military, and the law' is one which has been widely echoed by observers of the British scene [87, *92*].

One of the first was Matthew Arnold, who saw a dangerous gap opening up between the professions, civilized and humanized through their admission to traditional forms of culture, and the 'philistine' commercial and industrial classes. Arnold's plan was to spread sweetness and light to the whole middle class through state secondary schools. Although this did not happen, statistics on students' backgrounds show that from around 1870 both public schools and ancient universities saw an influx from wealthy business families [64; 24; 142]. But a gap remained between this gentrified élite and the bulk of the middle class.

The significance of these changes is perhaps a matter of emphasis. There is general agreement that by 1900 there was a newly consolidated élite incorporating the upper business and professional strata, with a fusion of gentlemanly and bourgeois values. But did the traditional elements remain in control, admitting a selected quantity of new blood to be socialized into its own values, or (as others would argue) should the reform of public schools and universities be seen rather as a middle-class takeover, in which national institutions were modernized and transformed, and the realities of power and influence changed hands? Many agreeable aristocratic trappings were retained to give a sense of continuity, but individual aristocrats now had to compete on equal terms [142]. The Arnoldian reformers themselves, after all, were mostly middle-class liberals who believed that they were creating a new élite qualified to hold power in an industrial and increasingly democratic society. And the assimilation of new wealth through traditional education was long seen as a good thing, ensuring social stability and continuity, maintaining cultural values in a materialist society, tempering plutocracy with aristocracy, and demonstrating the British genius for peaceful change. Only when British history ceased to be regarded as a success story was a hostile spotlight turned on the phenomenon.

The gentrification of the business class, and the prevalence of the professional ethos over the business of money-making, are central themes in Martin Wiener's thesis on the 'decline of the industrial spirit'. According to Wiener, liberal education had created by the end of the nineteenth century 'a remarkably homogeneous and cohesive elite', whose shared outlook, adapted from the values of the landed class, 'marked a crucial rebuff for the social revolution begun by industrialization' [148, *11–12*]. This élite, profoundly antipathetic to the industrial activities on which Britain's wealth and power were based, presided over the twentieth-century decline of both. The process was part of a widely noted British (or perhaps only English) cultural complex which included nostalgia for rural life, the cult of the country house, the absorption of business families into the country gentry, and more recently the growth of then 'heritage' industry. The 'Wiener thesis', though criticized by professional historians, has enjoyed great vogue in political and journalistic circles, as have the ideas of

Correlli Barnett, who has argued that education gave the British élite a set of idealistic values, based on the Arnold-Jowett ethos of public service, which led it first to pursue great-power illusions beyond Britain's economic capacity to sustain, then after the Second World War to devote the nation's resources to the construction of the welfare state instead of the modernization of the economy [20; 21]. Barnett's ideas are interesting because they turn attention to the quality of Britain's political and administrative leadership, making unfavourable comparisons with other European countries. But it is the economic side of the question which has stimulated debate.

Wiener and Barnett come to similar conclusions to Anderson and Mayer, though from a very different political perspective; their ideas attracted attention in the 1980s because they suited the neo-liberal political mood which favoured entrepreneurial values over the ethos of public service [102]. But they also draw on a long history of criticism of the deficiencies of British technical education. This concern, inspired by fears of foreign competition, can be traced back to the 1860s, and underlay a series of official inquiries in the late nineteenth century. The apostles of 'national efficiency' in the 1900s were saying much the same as Barnett, and for them as for him it was Germany which provided the model of state-directed modernization. The criticism of Arnoldian culture also has many precedents, including the 'two cultures' controversy of the 1960s between C. P. Snow, spokesman for science, and the literary critic F. R. Leavis.

There are really two separate arguments in this debate. One (Snow's original point) is that science and technology do not have an adequate part in the general education of the British élite, leading ill-informed politicians and civil servants to give a low priority to questions of industrial production. This is a difficult argument to refute, given the undoubted prestige of arts education over the years, and the small percentage of science graduates to be found in most élite groups. Some might trade this deficiency back to the failure of Victorian propagandists like Huxley to get science accepted as a part of general culture rather than a vocational specialism; others might seek a less remote explanation in the early specialization which has been a feature of English secondary education since the Second World War.

The second argument points to the inadequate higher technical education of Britain's industrial leadership. The neglect of technology and engineering, the low prestige of technical institutions compared with universities, the reluctance of employers to spend money on training or to appreciate the importance of research and theory, the cult of the 'practical man' trained by shopfloor experience, the failure of companies to put engineers and other trained experts on their boards, the parsimony of the state and its refusal to adopt coherent educational strategies – these have been constant themes both with science and technology lobbies over the years, and in studies of this aspect of educational history [113; 114].

Universities are only part of the story, for technical education has also been neglected at lower levels. Sanderson, for example, has argued that the failure to develop a technical stream in secondary education has been a crucial British fault, reflecting the 'academic' bias encouraged by the demands of university entrance [125]. At the higher level, the negative case has been strongly restated by authors with a comparative perspective like Göran Ahlström and Robert Locke. By French and German standards, Britain simply produced too few science and engineering graduates. On the eve of the First World War, there were some 2700 full-time degree students in engineering and technology in English universities and technical colleges, compared with four times the number in the much-admired German 'technical high schools' [16; 2; 75; 76]. Locke has also argued that, while British employers remained congenitally suspicious of theoretical approaches of all kinds, in Germany higher education played a vital role in the development of management science and the transformation of entrepreneurship.

Economic historians have had much to say about the quality of British entrepreneurship, and the attitudes of businessmen towards their own education are relevant to this debate. The Mayer/Wiener argument is that, seduced by the glamour of tradition, they sent their sons to public schools and Oxbridge, where they learned to look down on the vulgarities of trade and production, and were diverted away from business careers. Thus the energies of the entrepreneurial class were sapped through a 'haemorrhage of talent'. It would have been better, from this point of view, if they had remained philistines. D. C. Coleman has pointed out that if the sons of businessmen did move into the professions, this at least created room for new talent in business. But he agrees that British industry suffered from a deadly combination of liberally-trained gentlemen in the boardroom and practical men on the factory floor, both hostile to trained scientific expertise [32]. We shall look again in Chapter 4 at the education of the business élite.

The economic charges against British education have often rested on sweeping generalizations, and have been treated most sceptically by those with most knowledge of educational history. Two recent critics of the Wiener thesis are Sidney Pollard, in a wide-ranging review of the whole question of decline [100], and Michael Sanderson. Sanderson's 1972 study of universities and industry, which took a broadly favourable view of the relations between the two, remains the most thorough study of any aspect of modern British university history, and he has recently returned to the attack [122; 126]. Some of the arguments used by Pollard are not related directly to education. Like a number of economic historians, he challenges the notion of a general economic decline before 1914, and points out that many sectors of the British economy, notably international commerce and finance, were very successful – and public school and Oxbridge men were more likely to be found in these sectors than in manufacturing. Whatever the validity of Wiener's analysis of British culture, it can be argued that he fails to prove a causal link with economic performance, or to provide a convincing chronological framework. Britain's un-doubted economic problems have been most acute since 1945, long after the heyday of liberal education, and despite substantial investment in scientific and technical education. The classics, the butt of so much criticism from Barnett and others, have practically vanished from schools and universities without any discernible benefit to the economy.

It is also easy for Pollard to show that the prestige of the classics, the professions and the civil service were no less strong in economically successful countries. While British historians have admired Germany, German ones have spoken of its 'tenacious anti-industrial value system' [67, *407*]. The desire to join the traditional élite was a common bourgeois trait, and the wealthy like to buy the best of everything, in education and social status for their children as in houses and lifestyles. Moreover it is not clear, even in Britain, that the low prestige of business should be taken as accepted fact. Since Victorian times there has been a cult of the heroic entrepreneur, and successful businessmen have not lacked access to political power and honours. Money is in any case its own reward, and the cult of the gentleman was perhaps only a consolatory ideology for ill-paid if well-educated professional men.

The main argument of defenders of the British record is that universities did in fact respond successfully to the scientific and technical revolution, and that the training of scientific experts and the pursuit of practical research joined older notions of liberal and professional education in a reinvigorated university ideal [18]. Oxbridge was slow to embrace vocationalism, but the civic colleges saw themselves from the start as 'community service stations' for their localities [17], welcoming new and practical subjects, and retaining a close involvement in technical and adult education. Down to the 1950s, the redbrick image was one of utilitarian colleges situated in grimy industrial towns. Far from being pale Oxbridge imitations, they were 'a prime expression of the industrial spirit, closely linked with industry, drawing their life-blood finance from it, and pumping back research and students to it' [126, *103*]. Sanderson's 1972 research showed that by 1900 many graduates did go into industry, and in Britain (unlike Germany) engineering and applied science were accepted as university subjects from an early date – though there is legitimate debate about which was the more effective pattern, for Locke and others argue that higher technical instruction was better given in separate institutions. Pollard takes an even more optimistic view than Sanderson, arguing that there was no real underdevelopment of technical education, since the British system of learning on the job, or informally through evening classes and private study for professional examinations, was well suited to a country with a long heritage of industrial experience and to the particular industries in which Britain was strong. This argument, confined to the period before 1914, seems less valid for later years, when innovation and modernization were the first priority, and perhaps underestimates the stigma which part-time or non-degree study stamped on technical education in a system where the residential university enjoyed so much prestige.

Pollard also points to the 'astonishingly vigorous expansive phase in the decades before the First World War' [100, *175*], and argues that Britain was rapidly catching up with Germany until the interruption of war. The complaints of the science and national efficiency lobbies had produced action, including new levels of state funding, and initiatives like the foundation of Imperial College, whose constituent parts already had an impressive record as centres of technological expertise [16]. The output of science graduates greatly increased, and outside Oxford and Cambridge arts graduates were in a minority. Oxford admittedly lagged behind [61], but Cambridge became a major centre for scientific research and teaching; while classics and history remained the most popular subjects at Oxford, at Cambridge these were natural science, classics, and mathematics, in that order – an example of how generalizations about 'Oxbridge' can be misleading [112; 114].

But there was also a less encouraging side to the picture. Whatever the significance of government grants, the civic universities were never financially secure, and relied on private funding for new chairs, laboratories and other capital expenditure [114]. This was often forthcoming, but from a limited number of individuals and families, and from private fortunes rather than the corporate funds of local firms. Gifts might reflect the donor's interest in cultural causes rather than industrial or commercial needs; at one point Liverpool had four chairs of archaeology, all funded by shipping and industrial families [70]. There were cases where universities developed specialities in fruitful cooperation with local industry, as with chemistry at Manchester, textiles at Leeds, mining at Newcastle, or metallurgy at Sheffield, but there were other industries – hosiery at Nottingham, coal at Cardiff, textiles and shipbuilding at Belfast – which conspicuously failed to support their local college. Generally speaking, the industrial link was firmest in the north of England, and weakest in Wales, whose 'culture was inimical to the advancement of science, technology and commerce' [115, *442*]. In Scotland, the traditional orientation towards the professions meant less pressure to adapt to new needs, and the one foundation of a 'civic' type, Dundee, was soon affiliated with St Andrews. Glasgow did develop effective teaching in engineering and naval architecture, but both Glasgow and Edinburgh also had independent technical colleges which were able to exploit fields left untouched by the universities [110].

The final argument in defence of the universities' record is that 'the more insidious evil has not been anti-industrial attitudes in the universities so much as anti-intellectual, anti-academic attitudes in industry' [126, *102*]. The problem was not that the leaders and middle ranks of business had too much 'liberal' education, but that they had too little education of any kind. Despite the early development of engineering courses, the engineering profession itself was slow to accept them. Within industry, prejudices against pure theory died hard, and there were in any case few salaried posts for scientists, or for professional managers until corporate organization replaced family control. The universities probably did as much as they could in the conditions of the time, and there were many examples of attempts to introduce new subjects failing because of the indifference of employers. This was especially the case in commerce. As early as the 1880s, there were experiments with business courses based on economics, geography, law and similar subjects, and by 1914 several universities had faculties of commerce (notably Birmingham, but it was not unique). These efforts generally failed to win over employers, who believed that men should enter an office at sixteen or seventeen and work their way up. One successful exception was the railway department at the London School of Economics – but railways were ahead of most commercial bodies in adopting modern management techniques.

What universities were able to achieve depended on the nature of the actual demand for higher education, and their capacity for influence was thus limited. Education reflects the culture and values of a society as much as it moulds them, and one cannot isolate its effects from the other elements of complex social and economic phenomena. It does seem valid to say that the ancient universities (and the public schools) gave the topmost British élite a recognizable set of common values, with elements which may be called aristocratic or pre-industrial. These values had their own function in ensuring social stability and forming the political and administrative leadership of an imperial nation. That they spread to the middle class generally, and had a significant effect on economic performance, is easier to assert than to prove, and scepticism seems especially justified when university education was an option chosen by only a small part of the middle and even the upper classes. For as the next chapter will show, until recently the connexion of university education with élite positions was far from universal.

# 4

# Origins and destinations

Much university history is uninformative about the social function of universities. It elaborates on the history of institutions and curricula, and the scholarly achievements and ideals of professors, without paying much attention to the students without whom there would not be a university at all. But the expansion of higher education since 1800 can only be explained by looking at demand as well as supply: why did it come to seem increasingly valuable, eventually perhaps indispensable, to students and their parents? The study of students' origins (their class and family backgrounds) and destinations (the links between universities and occupations) gives some statistical backing to theories about professionalization, the formation of élites, or social mobility.

Professionalization is perhaps the most widely accepted explanatory theory, and for England it owes much to the work of Harold Perkin, who has argued in two books [95; 97] that the professional idea of 'trained expertise and selection by merit' first challenged and then overcame its rivals, the aristocratic ideal based on land and birth, and the entrepreneurial ideal based on capital. In analysing the 'decline of the entrepreneurial ideal' [95] and the rise of the professional ethos, Perkin resembles the theorists of middle-class failure, but with a significant difference of emphasis, for he sees professionalism itself, based on merit and competition, as essentially middle-class. It has spread, he argues, from the original professions to embrace first the expanding state machinery of bureaucracy, education and welfare, then the corporatized business world.

In this interpretation universities have a key role as the source of credentials for the meritocratic élite and the guarantors of professional expertise, and according to Perkin 'between 1850 and 1930 there took place in England a revolution in higher education . . . nothing less than the transformation of the university from a marginal institution, an optional finishing school for young gentlemen, into the central power house of modern industrial society'. Formal education replaced apprenticeship and other informal modes of recruitment, and universities became the focus for hopes of social advancement and 'the normal route to high status and income. This was an aspect of the rise of professionalism as the guiding principle of modern society' [Perkin in 63, *207, 218*]. Although 1930 may be too early for the completion of the process, this was undoubtedly the direction of development.

But how widespread was the experience of university? As we have seen, the percentage of the age-group involved was less than 1 per cent before 1914, and had only reached 3–4 per cent in the 1950s. This was far less than the proportion of the middle class, however defined, in the population. Such figures might be explained if universities were attended only by the topmost strata of society, but we know that this was not the case. Students came from all social classes, but in very different proportions. Here we can make use of modern studies based on interviewing large numbers of people about their educational experiences. One such study in the 1950s showed that among men born before 1910 university attendance was on average 2.1 per cent, but ranging from 11.9 per cent in the top two social categories (professional and managerial) to 0.5 per cent in the lowest two (semi-skilled and unskilled workers); among those born after 1910, the average was 3.7 per cent, ranging from 18 per cent to 1 per cent [J. Floud in 45, *137*). A study in the 1970s, using slightly different social categories, showed that for those born in 1943–52 the average had risen to 8.5 per cent, ranging from 26.4 per cent to 3.1 per cent [56, *264*]. These studies illustrate the trend of social inequality, as we shall see in Chapter 5; the point to note here is that even at the top of society university attendance has been a minority experience.

This should be borne in mind when looking at another type of evidence, 'élite studies' which examine the social and educational backgrounds of selected élite groups. These have some weaknesses. The élites chosen tend to be professional and official ones of the kind featured in directories, and it was here that graduates were most numerous. Elite studies also (by definition) look at those at the top of particular professions, who may not have been representative of the whole. A notable example are Church of England bishops, almost all of whom continued to be Oxbridge men long after the clergy as a whole had ceased to be [K. Thompson in 140]. Elite studies are most problematic in the business world, for they usually look at bankers, chairmen or company directors, and rarely at professional managers, or the entrepreneurs who ran the small businesses and family firms which were so large a part of the economy.

Another problem is that these studies cover, at the latest, those who reached top positions by the 1960s or 1970s, and do not reflect the recent expansion of higher education. Nevertheless, their findings have a striking uniformity: of those élite members who attended universities, the great majority (over 70 per cent in most cases, and often more) were at Oxford or Cambridge. There are usually appreciable numbers from London and the Scottish universities, but few from the redbricks. This is itself highly significant, showing that the top people in a wide range of occupations – politics, administration, the church, law, the armed services, the City of London, the higher ranks of industry – formed an unusually coherent national élite, integrated by a common educational background and dominated by a metropolitan culture [25; F. and J. Wakeford in 140].

Elite studies also commonly underline the dominance of the public schools, especially the leading ones, and their nexus with Oxbridge has generally led to the conclusion that the 'establishment' had a stranglehold over British life and that the citadels of power and influence were not easily stormed. The 'old boy network', and the clubs and other all-male institutions which prolonged the collegiate ethos in adult life, conspired to keep outsiders outside. But schooling was probably a more important and accurate indicator of social status than university education, for one finding of élite studies is that many élite members were not graduates at all; even in the 1950s, the average proportion of boys going to Oxbridge from the top twenty public schools was only a third, compared with a quarter in the 1860s [24, *124–5*].

Graduation rates naturally varied between different élites. One

much-studied example is politics. In 1906 57 per cent of Conservative MPs were graduates, and this figure did not rise substan-
tially until the 1950s; in 1987 it was 70 per cent. The growth of the
Labour party meant an influx of non-graduates in the early years,
though by 1987 56 per cent of Labour MPs were graduates [56,
*318*; cf. 50]. Politics, and some allied professions like journalism,
have remained relatively open to those without higher education.
The same may be said of the business élite, where studies show
quite a low percentage of graduates – commonly between 30 per
cent and 50 per cent even among leading groups like chairmen and
directors. (This is likely to have changed in recent years, as
professionalization has caught up with business, business studies
courses have multiplied in universities and polytechnics, and
employers have made a habit of recruiting graduates.) Comparisons also suggest that British businessmen were less well
qualified than their equivalents in other countries [R. Whitley,
and Stanworth and Giddens, in 140; 104; 67; 42].

Some business sectors embraced gentrification more strongly
than others – notably banking and finance, and some large-scale
industries like steel [41; 31]. When educational patterns are
studied in detail, the career paths of technocrats, self-made entrepreneurs and hereditary owners have to be distinguished, and
even established business families had different educational habits.
Some used Oxbridge for liberal education, especially second or
third generation families following the conventional habits of the
rich. But others trained their sons in science or economics, and
used civic universities or higher technical schools with a reputation
in a special field, perhaps combined with an engineering apprenticeship. It would be difficult to link specific cases with entrepreneurial success or failure, and since liberal higher education did
not as a matter of fact dominate the education of businessmen, it is
hard to blame it for sapping the industrial spirit [42; 65; 12]. The
'haemorrhage of talent' argument is also questionable, since universities were not seen as a normal preparation for business. It is
true that the percentage of business 'origins' was much higher than
that of business 'destinations' among graduates, but this may well
have been balanced by a reverse movement from the professions
into business, in which university education was not involved. For
the study of business élites also casts doubt on the notion of a

cultural divide within the middle class, at least after the pioneering days of entrepreneurialism. Business and professional families acted in much the same way, regarding the whole range of middle-class careers as open to their sons and making their educational choices accordingly.

One of the most systematic recent studies is a sample of over 3000 holders of élite posts between 1880 and 1970 which has been used by both Perkin [96; 97] and Rubinstein, though neither has published it fully. Some of the results of this, as shown by Rubinstein, are summarized in Table 4.1. Rubinstein [120] argues that élite studies too readily take attendance at a public school or Oxbridge as evidence of privileged status, and that British élites were recruited from comparatively wide backgrounds. Public schools were used by a wide range of middle-class families, and were the means by which the Victorian reforms succeeded in creating a meritocracy. Perkin [96] draws a similar conclusion – that there was a revolution of social mobility within the upper and middle classes, as the aristocracy lost ground and the older public schools had to share their privileges with the newer and less exclusive ones. The argument should not be pushed too far, for even the newer public schools were expensive and socially selective, putting a sharp limit on this meritocracy. But while Oxford and Cambridge continued to dominate élite recruitment, their own eventual opening to the grammar schools and the working classes meant real social change behind the façade of continuity.

This seems to be the lesson of Table 4.1. While the graduation rate rose, and Oxbridge dominance showed little change, the proportion of civil servants, bishops and vice-chancellors from public schools declined, as did those with 'élite origins' (Rubinstein's category, basically indicating family links with the landed class). By the 1960s some 40 per cent of these groups were coming from the lower middle and working classes. The pattern was different for industrialists, however, and Rubinstein's is not the only study to suggest that the top ranks of industry are among the most closed of British élites.

It should not be surprising that the civil service has been fairly meritocratic, since its competitive examinations (once including the Indian Civil Service) have always had high prestige as a goal for academic high-flyers [107]. R. K. Kelsall's studies [71; and in 140]

Table 4.1 *Characteristics of selected élite groups (in percentages)*

|  | 1880–99 | 1900–19 | 1920–39 | 1940–59 | 1960–70 |
|---|---|---|---|---|---|
| *Higher civil servants* | | | | | |
| Graduates | 58 | 73 | 85 | 86 | 89 |
| At Oxbridge | 44 | 57 | 66 | 61 | 71 |
| At public schools | 58 | 56 | 47 | 46 | 40 |
| Elite origins | 51 | 26 | 18 | 8 | 12 |
| From social classes I–III | 98 | 95 | 89 | 84 | 57 |
| From social classes IV–VII | 2 | 5 | 11 | 16 | 43 |
| *Bishops* | | | | | |
| Graduates | 100 | 94 | 100 | 98 | 100 |
| At Oxbridge | 96 | 94 | 98 | 90 | 80 |
| At public schools | 61 | 68 | 72 | 54 | 40 |
| Elite origins | 36 | 20 | 13 | 6 | 0 |
| From social classes I–III | 100 | 94 | 91 | 78 | 61 |
| From social classes IV–VII | 0 | 6 | 9 | 22 | 39 |
| *University vice-chancellors* | | | | | |
| Graduates | 100 | 98 | 98 | 100 | 91 |
| At Oxbridge | 81 | 83 | 70 | 80 | 62 |
| At public schools | 73 | 71 | 55 | 44 | 47 |
| Elite origins | 17 | 8 | 0 | 3 | 0 |
| From social classes I–III | 92 | 92.5 | 80 | 74 | 56 |
| From social classes IV–VII | 8 | 7.5 | 20 | 26 | 44 |
| *Industrialists* | | | | | |
| Graduates | | 15 | 26 | 35 | 64 |
| At Oxbridge | | 9 | 21 | 21 | 45 |
| At public schools | | 32 | 47 | 54 | 57 |
| Elite origins | | 25 | 28 | 17 | 22 |
| From social classes I–III | | 84 | 86 | 83 | 68 |
| From social classes IV–VII | | 16 | 14 | 17 | 32 |

*Source:* [120].

suggest that, despite the many social biases in the selection process, the examination system achieved its original aim of opening the service to the upper middle class and (rather less effectively) broadened recruitment further in the twentieth century. As for the academic profession, which only became recognizable as such at the end of the nineteenth century, the dons at post-reform Oxbridge came from the same upper middle class as the bulk of their students [40], while in Scotland early professionalization meant that professors were always predominantly middle class, with a smaller admixture from the lower classes than the democratic myth might lead one to expect [10]. Later development seems to have been in the same direction as Rubinstein's vice-chancellors, for surveys in the 1960s found 30 per cent or more of university teachers from the lower middle and working classes [94; 54].

Thus despite the undoubted dominance of the reformed public schools and ancient universities, those who used them were not a narrow élite. Their staple clientele included the children of clergy-men, solicitors, army officers, civil servants, professors, and other modest professionals, along with a wealthier element from the country gentry, business and the rentier class. Families with little capital could give their sons an education which would ensure social status and occupational security, and such men formed the backbone of the late Victorian and Edwardian public services and intelligentsia. It was the world of E. M. Forster's novels. One strength of the British system was that families who could afford this sort of education, however new their wealth or provincial their origins, found a direct route to the heart of the national culture and to the 'glittering prizes' of law and politics – a phrase popularized by the politician F. E. Smith, a prime example of the phenomenon. Later a handful of working-class scholars enjoyed the same advan-tage. But most Oxbridge graduates had to be content with more modest professional positions, and as elsewhere many were ab-sorbed by teaching.

The composition of the student body at Oxford and Cambridge is well documented by the studies of Stone and Jenkins and Jones, which are corroborated by figures from individual colleges [116; 49]. According to Lawrence Stone, Oxford reached a peak of social exclusiveness in the second quarter of the nineteenth century, but opened up after 1860 as 'Oxford at last adapted itself to the values and aspirations of the bourgeoisie'. Between 1870 and 1910 the sons of landowners declined from 40 per cent to 15 per cent and of the clergy from 28 per cent to 17 per cent, while those of other professional men rose from 21 per cent to 31 per cent and of businessmen from 7 per cent to 21 per cent. The aristocracy were 'swamped by a great tide of students from the new middle classes, professional, commercial, industrial, and white collar, the upper ranks of whom had been culturally and ethically assimilated by the common experience of education in a public school'. Thus although by 1900 'a few lower middle-class children were beginning to creep in once more, and there were even one or two children from the working class', the middle classes were the great beneficiaries of reform [142, *65, 67, 74, 103*].

It was a similar if slower story at Cambridge. In 1800–49, 32 per cent of the students were the sons of clergymen and 31 per cent of landowners; most of the rest came from the professions, with only 6 per cent from business. In 1850–99, the sons of landowners had fallen to 19 per cent and those of businessmen risen to 15 per cent, but sons of the clergy were still 31 per cent. It was not until the twentieth century that real change took place: in a 1937–8 sample only 2 per cent of the parents were landowners and 7 per cent clergymen, while 46 per cent were now in business, and 31 per cent of the students themselves went into business, compared with 7 per cent in 1850–99 and none before that. The proportion from public schools, which reached a remarkably high 82 per cent in 1850–99, fell only to 73 per cent in 1937–8; figures for Oxford would be similar [64]. This underlines that it was an invasion of the new middle classes, not the meritocratic masses, one aspect being that the college scholarships, originally designed for the poor, now mostly went to public-school candidates.

The social diversification of Oxford and Cambridge was a slow process, but other universities, with their local recruitment and relatively low fees, offered greater opportunities for social mobility. Thus according to Sanderson, by 1900 the system as a whole was coming to assume its modern role as the 'fire and crucible of social change and mobility' [123, *20*]. The extent of this has been concealed by a tendency to cite the Oxbridge data as if they were typical of all English or even British students, which clearly they were not [4; 68; Jarausch in 63]. The new colleges in London and the provinces were middle-class from the start. Outside Oxbridge, details of student backgrounds are unfortunately rare, but a survey at Owens College in 1867 found that 65 per cent were 'sons of merchants, manufacturers, professionals, and persons of independent means'. At Birmingham in 1893, similar groups accounted for 53 per cent, with 34 per cent from the lower middle class and

13 per cent from the 'artisan working class' [66, *153*; 125, *43*]. And there is evidence that by 1914, with the growth of local authority scholarships and teacher training, the 'ladder' of opportunity from the elementary schools gave colleges like Nottingham, Liverpool or Leeds a substantial body of working-class students [12]. If more data were available, the social character of these universities might look very like their Scottish and Welsh equivalents. As there, many students went into teaching (in state schools rather than the public schools favoured by Oxbridge graduates) and poorer students came more from the lower middle and skilled working classes than the ranks of unskilled labour. At this social level, too, the world of H. G. Wells rather than E. M. Forster, technical colleges and evening classes might have more appeal than conventional universities, and play as large a part in social mobility.

In some cases, we can link the social origins of individual students directly with their careers, which prove to be conditioned by family background. On one hand, professions like law and medicine had a strong element of continuity from father to son. On the other, poorer students tended to go into the church or teaching, where it was easier to find a post on merit alone [64; Kelsall in 45; 11]. For a university degree was never an automatic passport to success. There were many careers where personal contacts and influence still mattered, and the costs of establishment went beyond education itself to include the purchase of practices or partnerships, apprenticeship premiums, or support in the ill-paid early years.

The educational calculations made by families were thus complex, and different choices were made about schooling and higher education. It may be useful to think of a 'middle-class leaving age' for full-time education – usually running five years or so ahead of the working-class leaving age – after which continuation became an option. In the early nineteenth century, this age was fifteen or sixteen, and only those sent to the traditional public schools regularly stayed longer. By 1914 the age was seventeen or eighteen, for girls as well as boys. All families of middle-class status would expect to give their children a secondary education, and by that time a public school was *de rigueur* in certain social milieux, though the development of grammar schools had also opened up a much wider choice for middle-class families, especially in the provinces. But to continue education after 18 was an expensive option. We may distinguish three broad patterns. Among the traditional and wealthy élite, where career choices were not an immediate priority, the university was likely to be Oxford or Cambridge, chosen for social reasons: for its critics, Oxford was still 'a playground for the sons of the wealthier classes' [cited by Lowe in 92]. At this level, universities endorsed the power of birth and capital, and added a cultural polish, but were not themselves the instrument of élite formation. And even in this class, many men – those destined for the army, for example – were not sent to a university. Secondly, there were the general ranks of the middle class. Here, a university education would be seen as an investment, chosen only where appropriate to the intended career. If that career was business, university education would not be a normal choice, unless a specific technical preparation was sought. Third came the small number of students from the lower middle or working class, who reached university through exceptional luck, talent or determination; their choice of university was likely to be constrained by what scholarships were available.

Family plans were also conditioned by gender, and this is one way of approaching the history of higher education for women. Long seen in terms of heroic pioneers, recent historians have emphasized that it should be related to the general history of middle-class educational change; the pioneers themselves often came from upper middle class families with strong educational connexions [93; 146; 143; 36]. Teaching had always been an important occupation for women, and like other professions it was now put on a new academic basis in response to the formalization and institutionalization of schooling. In addition, of course, the movement reflected changes in the conception of women's social role, for career pressures had limited effects when so few professions were open to women. Historians of girls' secondary education have stressed that the demand for intellectual equality was compatible with the traditional idea of 'separate spheres', and that many headmistresses had quite conservative ideas about preparing for marriage and motherhood. Secondary schooling for girls became an uncontroversial convention. But this was much less true of higher education, where activists like Emily Davies at

Cambridge had strong feminist views. Choosing to go to college often meant leaving home, and rejecting family values in favour of an independent career. Many women were forced by circumstances to equip themselves to make an independent living; but alongside them in the women's colleges could be found a more leisured clientele attracted by scholarly ideals, and perhaps by the idea of forming distinctively female communities [146].

Such colleges, at Oxbridge and London, may have attracted undue historical attention. Most women who went to universities joined mixed institutions; University College London, it has been pointed out, was the largest 'women's' college in England [144]. University women had similar social backgrounds to men – the professional and business classes at Oxbridge, the middle to lower classes in Scotland – but with fewer either from the upper classes (where there was little thought of women having careers) or the working class (where both the scholarship machinery and the psychology of motivation traditionally favoured boys) [7; 11; 146; 62; 143; 90]. Once arrived, women found many problems of adjustment and acceptance, and the separate college system at Oxbridge, combined with overt discrimination, long prevented women playing their full part in university life. Elsewhere they eventually became accepted, though not perhaps until after 1900, as an integral part of the student body, and in many arts faculties they formed the majority [85; 57; 90].

Teaching was by far the commonest career, indeed the only profession fully open to women before 1914. This made women's higher education especially dependent on the fluctuations of demand for teachers, and put an upper limit on its expansion. Despite the struggle to enter medicine, many medical schools, including the leading ones in London, remained closed to women, and even when they qualified there were further barriers to progress in medical careers [3]. After 1918 professions like law and the civil service were opened to women, but the churches remained closed, as did most responsible posts in industry and commerce. Thus very few women ever reached the kind of positions covered by élite studies.

The change in women's status since the 1960s has been one component of the revolution in higher education. But there has been another movement of equal significance: the raising of the middle-class leaving age. As late as the 1950s, universities were far from being the chief distributors of élite jobs and status. University education was linked with a set of 'professional' careers, and its appeal diminished, as in the 1930s, if the outlets seemed to be shrinking. University expansion, including the limited extension of social mobility before 1914, was due partly to the rise of low-status professions like teaching. Graduation was not in itself a mark of bourgeois status (as in Germany), nor did failure to attend college carry any stigma (as was becoming the case in America). In business, in the landed class, in politics, it could easily be dispensed with. But all this was to change when graduation became the road to the general range of middle-class jobs. Once university education became in effect free, the costs of professional training were loaded from parents and the professions themselves onto the state. Middle-class families could hardly afford not to take up this offer, and it therefore became general to aim at extending full-time education to 21 or 22. Three or four years of higher education became a normal part of middle-class experience, and the concept of the 'graduate' replaced the older professional idea. This movement accounted for a large part of the post-war expansion, and helped to ensure that equality of opportunity proved a more elusive aim than had been expected.

# 5
# Elites and masses

Between the end of the nineteenth century and the 1950s, the character of British higher education remained stable. It was stratified, with universities of different types meeting different social and regional needs. It trained for the limited number of professions seen as appropriate for graduates. It was not generally selective, for demand rarely exceeded supply, and entrance examinations were qualifying rather than competitive. Middle-class students whose parents paid fees rubbed shoulders with poorer ones aided by scholarships. Individual social mobility was quite widespread, but the system as a whole reflected the existing social structure.

The post-war reforms, in both secondary and higher education, were intended to change this by treating children of all social classes equally. The image of the 'ladder' climbed by talented individuals was replaced by the 'sieve', sifting out the talent of a whole generation [125]. Once grants for higher education became mandatory, social justice demanded that university entrance should become an impartial selection process depending on the '18+' – the Advanced Level and Scottish Higher examinations. Universities were treated as a single system, and the ability of wealthy parents to secure places by paying fees, especially at Oxbridge, disappeared. A new and significant difference thus emerged between higher education, where meritocratic principles were applied universally, and secondary, where the survival of the public and other independent schools allowed fee-paying parents to bypass the selective process.

University entrance also became more competitive because of rising demand. The post-war years saw two movements labelled

Table 5.1 *Students with fathers in manual occupations, 1955 (in percentages)*

|                  | Men | Women | All |
| ---------------- | --- | ----- | --- |
| Oxford           | 14  | 8     | 13  |
| Cambridge        | 10  | 5     | 9   |
| London           | 24  | 14    | 21  |
| Civic            | 34  | 24    | 31  |
| Wales            | 46  | 31    | 40  |
| Scotland         | 28  | 16    | 24  |
| Northern Ireland | 18  | 9     | 15  |
| UK               | 27  | 19    | 25  |

the 'bulge' (higher birth rates) and the 'trend' (higher staying-on rates at secondary schools). By the 1950s, despite recent expansion in response to perceived manpower needs, the supply of qualified students outran the available places, and the chances of entry were declining. This was the situation addressed by the Robbins report, and its fundamental argument was the need to bring places into line with demand.

The statistics compiled by Robbins revealed the prestige hierarchy bequeathed by historical development. Table 5.1 illustrates the differences in social composition, which were even more apparent when universities were compared with technical and teacher-training colleges, with 38 per cent and 40 per cent respectively of manual parents [109, Appendix 2B, 72, 92]. Social class was inevitably linked with schooling, and the same distinctions appeared: while the average proportion of male university students from independent schools was 25 per cent. Cambridge had 60 per cent and Oxford 53 per cent [109, Appendix 2B, 9).

The report was backed up by many contemporary surveys, part of a flourishing school of sociological inquiry which focused on social mobility and class inequalities in education. These topics had attracted attention even between the wars, but interest was at its height in the 1960s and 1970s, and many of the findings are available in convenient summaries or compendia [J. H. Farrant in 43; B. Williamson in 99; 103; 38; 55; 56; 125]. These sociologists – the preeminent expert on higher education is A. H. Halsey – can tell us as much as historians about post-war developments. Their work was characteristic of British sociology in its concern for empirical investigation and its direct influence on policy, especially in the 1960s, but sociology has also contributed some general theories about education and society which are helpful in understanding historical developments.

One important form of evidence was the sample studies already referred to in Chapter 4. These typically showed that middle-class children, broadly defined, were five or six times as likely as working-class children to reach a university. At the extremes of the social scale, the disparity was even greater. Robbins found, for example, that among higher professionals 33 per cent reached degree level, but among the children of semi-skilled and unskilled workers only 1 per cent [109, 50]. When gender was taken into account, inequalities were greater still, for at this period working-class women were markedly under-represented (see also Table 5.2 below).

These studies distinguished between different birth 'cohorts', and while they showed that university attendance was growing steadily, its distribution between the classes did not seem to have changed radically. Little and Westergaard concluded in 1964 that 'there are certainly no indications of any narrowing of class differentials in access to universities over the generations. . . . the social class composition of the student body in the universities has remained roughly the same during the past three to five decades' [74, 311]. And the main cohort study of the 1970s found that while in the professional and managerial classes university attendance rose from 7 per cent among those born in 1913–22 to 26 per cent among those born in 1943–52, for the working class the rise was proportionately slightly less – from 0.9 per cent to 3 per cent [56, 264].

University selection itself did not seem affected by class bias, for those selected were representative of those who applied; working-class children were succeeding in entering grammar schools, but falling by the wayside before reaching the university stage. Much research thus focused on inequalities of performance in secondary schools. Although the grammar schools were the 'academic' part of the tripartite system, they took about 20 per cent of the population at a time when universities took only 4 per cent. A large proportion of pupils left by 16, and there were great disparities in leaving rates between middle and working class children of equal ability. Many of the latter were in any case excluded by the 11+ selection, which despite its reliance on apparently objective intelligence testing was increasingly criticized for its premature judgements, unreliable predictive value, arbitrary local variations and hidden class biases. These problems – conveniently summarized in Sanderson's thorough survey of educational opportunity in the twentieth century [125] – formed part of the argument for comprehensive schools. It was hoped that non-selective education would put an end to the barriers which progressively excluded all but a small élite, increase the staying-on rate, and encourage diversity of choice.

The effects of this policy remain controversial, politically if not academically. In the 1940s and 1950s the grammar schools helped to create a wholly new demand for higher education, and produced a generation of men and women with non-élite backgrounds who had a very distinctive impact on British social, political and intellectual life. It has been claimed that their academic atmosphere stimulated and motivated working-class scholars in a way which comprehensive schools have not, and that the selective system was very effective at promoting social mobility: the proportion of working-class university students in the 1960s was high by international standards. In the grammar school era, the function of universities was seen as producing an élite of 'leaders' from a limited 'pool of ability', and it was commonly felt that only those who were unusually clever or 'bright' should go to university. This would certainly have surprised the dons of Victorian Oxbridge, used to dealing with upper-class 'passmen'; for it was meritocratic élitism, rather than the defence of traditional privilege, which inspired critics of university expansion like the 'Black Paper' contributors

How far has the expansion of numbers since the 1960s changed the class balance of the universities? The most readily available information is about the social origins of students, and Table 5.2 does not show any strong trend to democratization. There is a striking continuity, not only between the 1950s and the 1980s but with the kind of figures found in Scotland (and Wales) well before 1914. If anything, the figures for 1989, which are typical of the 1980s [56, *293*], suggest retrogression. In fact they reflect the shift

Table 5.2 *Social origins of university students (in percentages)*

| Social class: | I | II | IIIN | IIIM | IV | V |
|---|---|---|---|---|---|---|
| 1910, Glasgow | 19 | 39 | 10 | 23 | 8 | 1 |
| 1934, Glasgow | 18 | 39 | 12 | 20 | 9 | 3 |
| **1955, England** | | | | | | |
| Men | 22 | 41 | 11 | 22 | 4 | 1 |
| Women | 27 | 45 | 9 | 16 | 2 | 1 |
| **1955, Scotland** | | | | | | |
| Men | 19 | 41 | 12 | 22 | 5 | 1 |
| Women | 24 | 45 | 10 | 16 | 4 | 1 |
| **1955, Wales** | | | | | | |
| Men | 14 | 38 | 10 | 27 | 9 | 2 |
| Women | 17 | 46 | 11 | 20 | 5 | 1 |
| 1989, UK | 21 | 49 | 11 | 12 | 6 | 1 |

*Note:* Class I, higher professional and managerial; II, intermediate; IIIN, skilled non-manual; IIIM, skilled manual; IV, semi-skilled; V, unskilled.
*Sources:* [80]; [72, *Table 15*]; UCCA, *Statistical Supplement to the Twenty-Seventh Report, 1988–9* (Cheltenham, 1990).

towards middle-class occupations in the general population, but once the relative size of classes is allowed for the difference of opportunity between middle and working class children is still about five to one, and for Class I the APR has risen to 60 per cent or more [Anderson in 30]. Against this we should set the greater flexibility of career choices in a larger and more diverse system: working-class students are no longer directed into teaching by financial constraints, and have benefited from the expansion of the public sector. Statistical data for polytechnics are sparse, but one study in 1972–3 (including part-time students) found 12 per cent of parents in class I, 34 per cent in class II, 18 per cent in class IIIN, 8 per cent in class IIIM, 2 per cent in class IV, and 16 per cent in class V (with 10 per cent unclassified); thus polytechnics, unlike universities, seem to have done more for the unskilled than the skilled working class [43, *85*; cf. 103, *243*]. They also had less appeal to the middle classes, for the binary line has been social as well as functional; although the universities no longer dominate higher education as they did in the 1950s, within the university sector social opportunities have not been transformed by subsequent developments.

Thus judgements of the era of growth have often been critical. E. G. Edwards, in a polemical but well-documented plea for expansion, spoke of 'the persistence of social apartheid' [38]. Sanderson was more cautious, but nevertheless considered that 'entry to universities in spite of the Robbins expansion still remains restricted to a relatively small élite [125, *74*]. Halsey in 1986 was 'forced to the depressing conclusion that over the century so far, the unequal relative educational chances of boys from different class origins have been remarkably stable, and that the conventional picture of a steady trend towards equality has been an optimistic myth' [55, *134*]. And Roy Lowe asked, 'is the nature of the English education system . . . one key reason why elite groups have been able to retain most of their characteristics and many of the accompanying privileges?' He concluded that the system had responded to post-war social change by becoming the 'service industry' of new forms of stratification. 'Structural changes within the economy signalled the rise of a new middle class, the owner-occupiers who peopled the fast-growing suburbs. . . . Immediately after the war, an education system was devised which precipitated the creation of this social class. Its emergence ensured that, for the foreseeable future, England was to be a society which gave only a limited role to women, to the new ethnic minorities and to the working classes' [77, Introduction, *202*].

As this sentence suggests, there are other forms of bias besides the class inequalities to which British sociology has usually given priority [99; T. Blackstone in 98]. The under-representation of ethnic minorities is not a question which has been approached historically, but regional biases, particularly those in favour of London and the south-east [43; 77], would appear from Rubinstein's historical work to have a long history. The factor which has been most closely examined is gender, for while the proportion of women in higher education has risen, it remains unequally distributed between subjects, and historians have stressed that, as in the past, degrees are not automatic passports to occupational equality [Dyhouse in 1; Sutherland in 144]. For whatever influence education may have, it inevitably reflects and partly transmits the inequalities of the society in which it is embedded.

Sociology offers various explanatory frameworks for this phenomenon. One which has recently become popular is 'social closure', derived from Max Weber. This theory states that dominant groups in society use particular definitions of education, expressed in its structure and values, to defend their interests and exclude alternative claims. The idea is simple enough, but can be used fruitfully to explore the educational strategies of the Victorian professions, the institutionalization of discrimination against women, or the pervasive power of the Oxbridge ideal [Acker in 1; 29]. It can also be linked with the concepts of 'sponsored' and 'contest' mobility, which derive from an article of 1960 by R. H. Turner [reprinted in 53]. Turner argued that educational systems reflect the norms of social mobility within their society, and contrasted Britain (sponsored) with America (contest). Where contest mobility prevails, education is open-ended, students are encouraged to stay for as long as possible, and final occupational distribution is competitive. There is both high participation and a high rate of failure. But under sponsored mobility, the pre-existing élite chooses at an early stage the individuals it wishes to recruit, and uses education to socialize them into its values and prepare them for their role. The sponsorship model, which is not incompatible in practice with high levels of social mobility, does correspond to some striking features of the British system, such as the assimilative role of the gentleman ideal, the stress on character formation and the residential experience, the development of selection and scholarships since 1902 as a series of hurdles for winnowing out all but the academic élite, and the combination of rigorous university selection with a virtual guarantee of graduation once admitted. The notion of sponsorship has thus become a commonplace of debate, though it can be plausibly argued that Scotland displays more contest features than England [83].

Both social closure and sponsored mobility imply the existence of an élite more or less consciously manipulating the system to suit its interests. So, of course, does a conventional Marxist interpretation which sees education as a reflection of class, bound in a capitalist society to serve the interests of the controllers of capital. Since modern educational systems do not emerge spontaneously, but depend on legislation and state policy, they are indeed likely to reflect the balance of political and social power, with social change diverted into acceptable channels and entrenched interests granted immunity. But there are also less conscious forces of conservatism at work, and this is recognized by the theory of 'reproduction'.

This concept is applied to Britain in the recent work of Müller, Ringer and Simon [92], but derives from the French sociologist Pierre Bourdieu who (with J. C. Passeron) sought to explain the continuing dominance of bourgeois students despite expansion within an open-entry system. They distinguished between the 'inheritors' whose family background provides 'cultural capital' equipping them to move smoothly from school to university, and the 'scholars' who fight their way up against the barriers of custom and cultural privilege. The notion of cultural capital has won widespread acceptance as a way of explaining the inequalities which persist within formally meritocratic selection procedures, and Detlef Müller, in a related argument, defines meritocracy as a legitimating ideology for the dominant bourgeois groups, basing selection on seemingly neutral and rational grounds which actually enshrine a class-specific culture [92].

The idea of reproduction can also be related to the kind of occupational approach used in Chapter 4. Parents who are themselves of middle-class status will expect their children to enjoy the same advantages, and will use their knowledge of the system and their financial power to secure whatever education is necessary to ensure this. This is one of the engines of expansion, which has become self-reinforcing as the new university graduates of the 1960s and 1970s themselves become parents. But it also means that middle-class occupations have a strong 'inherited' element which limits the numbers to be admitted from below, a point which seems substantiated by the surprisingly stable composition of the student body. In Britain this is facilitated by the division between state and independent schools – the latter now including many old grammar schools which at one time received 'direct grants' from the state as well as girls' day schools and the traditional public school. The attention given to university entry and the high rate of examination success are probably the chief reason why parents are willing to pay for this expensive form of schooling, with the result that schools with 6–7 per cent of the secondary school population account for a quarter of university entrants [125, 9]. In theory, impartial university selection evens out the difference between state and independent schools, but since entry to the more prestigious universities, or to universities rather than the public sector, depends on the level of examination grades, the quality of secondary education makes a significant difference. It can be argued that the 18+ has replaced the 11+ as the crucial determinant of educational fortunes, and that the raising of the middle-class leaving age has simply pushed selectivity to a later stage without causing any revolution in relative chances. It is not clear, indeed, that the fundamental balance between the reproductive and the social-mobility or meritocratic functions of universities has changed since the early twentieth century, for even at a much lower level of access individual mobility could coexist with skewed class representation; as Rubinstein's work shows, individuals could go far once admitted to the system.

Judgements of these matters will depend on one's view of general social change in Britain. Has the growth of professionalization finally made class obsolete, as Perkin argues? Does it make sense any longer to speak of the middle or working classes, or of a dominant élite or establishment as it was once understood? Does the diversification of the middle class mean that, amid a huge graduate salariat, the traditional professions no longer have any distinct character or prestige? Many observers would now see a tripartite social structure, shaped like a pear rather than the traditional pyramid: at the top, a large and assured upper middle class, open as always to new money, which has come to take higher education for granted, and uses the school system to secure it; in the middle a broad amalgam of the middle and upper working classes, a group stressed by Lowe in his account of post-war history [77], and probably the one which has gained most from state education and the public financing of universities; and the remainder of the unskilled and socially deprived working class, concentrated in inner cities or peripheral housing estates where access to high-quality secondary schools is difficult, and culturally less disposed to seize educational opportunities than the old skilled working class from whom the classic scholarship children were drawn.

Within the university system, a hierarchy of prestige certainly survives, but since the 1960s it has been considerably flattened. Universities have become more uniform, as general economic and social trends have undermined the distinctiveness of Britain's regions and nations. Oxford and Cambridge have become more like other universities, significantly reducing their public-school bias, and equalizing chances for women (only 10–15 per cent of undergraduates in the 1950s) by abolishing single-sex colleges. They have not become either social ghettos for the wealthy or (as might also have happened) academic hothouses draining the best students away from elsewhere to form a national super-élite. This is largely the result of the mandatory grant system. But developments in university finance may again increase the distinction between universities, favouring those with historical glamour, international connexions and wealthy alumni.

Higher education is the most egalitarian part of British education, in being a unified public system with no private alternative, and in bringing together students of all classes on equal terms. In this it differs from the secondary sector – and also from the harsh world after graduation, for while degrees are in principle equal, in the eyes of employers some institutions are more equal than others. At present the meritocracy of higher education compensates for the inequalities of secondary schooling; the danger is that higher education might itself return to a pattern of private affluence and public mediocrity. The Robbins compromise between liberal ideals and democratic expansion relied on state intervention to counter this, and it was perhaps especially needed in a culture where the contest ideology was too weak to produce a strong popular demand for higher education. The power of the market, on the other hand, is likely to strengthen social inequalities by allowing wealth to be turned into cultural capital.

In the 1960s those who sought to modernize British society targeted the establishment and the 'old school tie', and saw privilege and inequality in education as obstacles to the formation of a democratically recruited, scientifically trained élite. By the 1980s this idea had gone out of fashion, and a new modernization project had appeared stressing utilitarianism and market-oriented, entrepreneurial values. Social justice and efficiency seemed to be rival ideals. But is this really the case? An élite which fails to draw able recruits from every part of the social spectrum, as is still the case in many areas of British life, may also rise inadequately to the challenges of social, political and economic change. Britain's success in meeting these challenges is not so self-evident as to justify complacency about the means by which its élite is chosen and trained.

# Bibliography

This bibliography is intended as a guide to scholarly work which has appeared since the 1950s. Most older books were histories of individual institutions, including colleges at Oxford, Cambridge and London. These have of course continued to appear, and many are of a high standard; but their focus is inevitably somewhat narrow, and with a few exceptions they have been excluded from the list below. One important project in course of publication is the official history of the University of Oxford, but at the time of writing the volumes covering the nineteenth and twentieth centuries had not appeared. Other universities with active historical projects include Aberdeen, Birmingham and Glasgow.

Those in search of further reading will find useful bibliographies, including older works, in the following: **General**: Sanderson, *The Universities in the Nineteenth Century*; Sanderson, *Education, Economic Change and Society in England, 1780–1870*; Kelly, *For Advancement of Learning: the University of Liverpool, 1881–1981*. **Scotland**: Anderson, *Education and Opportunity in Victorian Scotland: Schools and Universities*. **Wales**: Morgan, *Rebirth of a Nation: Wales, 1880–1980*. **Universities and industry**: Sanderson, *The Universities and British Industry, 1850–1970*; Pollard, *Britain's Prime and Britain's Decline: the British Economy, 1870–1914*. **Elites**: Boyd, *Elites and their Education*. **Women's education**: Delamont, *Knowledgeable Women: Structuralism and the Reproduction of Elites*. **Universities and opportunity**: Sanderson, *Educational Opportunity and Social Change in England*. An annual list of new work is published in the periodical *History of Universities*.

[1] Acker, S. and Piper, D. W. (1984) *Is Higher Education Fair to Women?* (Guildford).

[2] Ahlström, G. (1982) *Engineers and Industrial Growth. Higher Technical Education and the Engineering Profession during the Nineteenth and Early Twentieth Centuries: France, Germany, Sweden and England* (London).

[3]  Alexander, W. (1987) *First Ladies of Medicine: the Origins, Education and Destination of Early Women Medical Graduates of Glasgow University* (Glasgow).

[4]  Anderson, C. A. (1959) 'The Social Composition of University Student Bodies. The Recruitment of Nineteenth-Century Elites in Four Nations: a Historical Case Study', *The Year Book of Education.* [England, Germany, Russia, U.S.A.]

[5]  Anderson, P. (1964) 'Origins of the Present Crisis', *New Left Review*, No. 23.

[6]  ——, (1969) 'Components of the National Culture' in A. Cockburn and R. Blackburn (eds), *Student Power: Problems, Diagnosis, Action* (Harmondsworth).

[7]  Anderson, R. D. (1983) *Education and Opportunity in Victorian Scotland: Schools and Universities* (Oxford). [new edn with updated bibliography 1989]

[8]  —— (1985) 'In Search of the "Lad of Parts": the Mythical History of Scottish Education', *History Workshop*, No. 19.

[9]  —— (1985) 'Education and Society in Modern Scotland: a Comparative Perspective', *History of Education Quarterly*, xxv.

[10]  —— (1987) 'Scottish University Professors, 1800–1939: Profile of an Elite', *Scottish Economic and Social History*, vii.

[11]  —— (1988) *The Student Community at Aberdeen, 1860–1939* (Aberdeen).

[12]  —— (1991) 'Universities and Elites in Modern Britain', *History of Universities*, x.

[13]  Annan, N. (1955) 'The Intellectual Aristocracy' in J. H. Plumb (ed.), *Studies in Social History: a Tribute to G. M. Trevelyan* (London).

[14]  —— (1982) 'British Higher Education, 1960–80: a Personal Retrospect', *Minerva*, xx.

[15]  —— (1990) *Our Age: Portrait of a Generation* (London).

[16]  Argles, M. (1964) *South Kensington to Robbins: an Account of English Technical and Scientific Education since 1851* (London).

[17]  Armytage, W. H. G. (1955) *Civic Universities: Aspects of a British Tradition* (London).

[18]  Ashby, E. (1958) *Technology and the Academics: an Essay on the Universities and the Scientific Revolution* (London).

[19]  Ashby, E. and Anderson, M. (1974) *Portrait of Haldane at Work on Education* (London).

[20]  Barnett, C. (1972) *The Collapse of British Power* (London).

[21]  —— (1986) *The Audit of War: the Illusion and Reality of Britain as a Great Nation* (London).

[22]  Becher, H. W. (1984–5) 'The Social Origins and Post-Graduate Careers of a Cambridge Intellectual Elite, 1830–1860', *Victorian Studies*, xxviii.

[23] Bill, E. G. W. (1973) *University Reform in Nineteenth-Century Oxford: a Study of Henry Halford Vaughan, 1811–1885* (Oxford).

[24] Bishop, T. J. H. and Wilkinson, R. (1967) *Winchester and the Public School Elite: a Statistical Analysis* (London).

[25] Boyd, D. (1973) *Elites and their Education* (Windsor).

[26] Bryant, M. (1979) *The Unexpected Revolution: a Study in the History of the Education of Women and Girls in the Nineteenth Century* (Windsor).

[27] Cardwell, D. S. L. (1972) *The Organisation of Science in England* (2nd edn, London).

[28] Carswell, J. (1985) *Government and the Universities in Britain: Programme and Performance, 1960–1980* (Cambridge).

[29] Carter, L. (1990) *Ancient Cultures of Conceit: British University Fiction in the Post-War Years* (London).

[30] Carter, J. J. and Withrington, D. J. (eds) (1992) *Scottish Universities: Distinctiveness and Diversity* (Edinburgh).

[31] Cassis, Y. (1985) 'Bankers in English Society in the Late Nineteenth Century', *Economic History Review*, 2nd series XXXVIII.

[32] Coleman, D. C. (1973) 'Gentlemen and Players', *Economic History Review*, 2nd series XXVI.

[33] Cunningham, S. (1984) 'Women's Access to Higher Education in Scotland', *World Yearbook of Education 1984* (London).

[34] Davie, G. E. (1964) *The Democratic Intellect: Scotland and her Universities in the Nineteenth Century* (Edinburgh). [replaced the original edn of 1961]

[35] —— (1986) *The Crisis of the Democratic Intellect: the Problem of Generalism and Specialisation in Twentieth-Century Scotland* (Edinburgh).

[36] Delamont, S. (1989) *Knowledgeable Women: Structuralism and the Reproduction of Elites* (London).

[37] Edwards, E. G. and Roberts, I. J. (1979–80) 'British Higher Education: Long-Term Trends in Student Enrolment', *Higher Education Review*, XII.

[38] Edwards, E. G. (1982) *Higher Education for Everyone* (Nottingham).

[39] Ellis, E. L. (1972) *The University College of Wales, Aberystwyth, 1872–1972* (Cardiff).

[40] Engel, A. J. (1983) *From Clergyman to Don: the Rise of the Academic Profession in Nineteenth-Century Oxford* (Oxford).

[41] Erickson, C. (1959) *British Industrialists: Steel and Hosiery, 1850–1950* (Cambridge).

[42] Fidler, J. (1981) *The British Business Elite: its Attitudes to Class, Status and Power* (London).

[43] Fulton, O. (ed.) (1981) *Access to Higher Education* (Guildford).

[44] Garland, M. McM. (1980) *Cambridge Before Darwin: the Ideal of a Liberal Education, 1800–1860* (Cambridge).

[45]  Glass, D. V. (ed.) (1954) *Social Mobility in Britain* (London).

[46]  Gowan, P. (1987) 'The Origins of the Administrative Elite', *New Left Review*, No. 162.

[47]  Green, V. H. H. (1957) *Oxford Common Room: a Study of Lincoln College and Mark Pattison* (London).

[48]  —— (1969) *British Institutions: the Universities* (Harmondsworth)

[49]  —— (1979) *The Commonwealth of Lincoln College, 1427–1977* (Oxford).

[50]  Guttsman, W. L. (1963) *The British Political Elite* (London).

[51]  Haig, A. G. L. (1986) 'The Church, the Universities and Learning in Later Victorian England', *Historical Journal*, XXIX.

[52]  Hall, J. A. (1979) 'The Curious Case of the English Intelligentsia', *British Journal of Sociology*, XXX.

[53]  Halsey, A. H., Floud, J. and Anderson, C. A. (1961) *Education, Economy and Society: a Reader in the Sociology of Education* (London).

[54]  Halsey, A. H. and Trow, M. A. (1971) *The British Academics* (London).

[55]  Halsey, A. H. (1986) *Change in British Society* (3rd edn, Oxford).

[56]  —— (ed.) (1988) *British Social Trends since 1900: a Guide to the Changing Social Structure of Britain* (London).

[57]  Hamilton, S. (1983) 'The First Generations of University Women', in G. Donaldson (ed.), *Four Centuries: Edinburgh University Life, 1583–1983* (Edinburgh).

[58]  Harvie, C. (1976) *The Lights of Liberalism: University Liberals and the Challenge of Democracy, 1860–86* (London).

[59]  Heyck, T. W. (1982) *The Transformation of Intellectual Life in Victorian England* (London).

[60]  Hickox, M. S. (1986) 'Has there been a British intelligentsia?', *British Journal of Sociology*, XXXVII.

[61]  Howarth, J. (1987) 'Science Education in Late-Victorian Oxford: a Curious Case of Failure?', *English Historical Review*, CII.

[62]  Howarth, J. and Curthoys, M. (1987) 'The Political Economy of Women's Higher Education in Late Nineteenth and Early Twentieth-Century Britain', *Historical Research*, LX.

[63]  Jarausch, K. H. (ed.) (1983) *The Transformation of Higher Learning, 1860–1930: Expansion, Diversification, Social Opening and Professionalization in England, Germany, Russia and the United States* (Chicago). [essays on England by R. Lowe, S. Rothblatt, H. Perkin, A. Engel]

[64]  Jenkins, H. and Jones, D. C. (1950) 'Social Class of Cambridge University Alumni of the 18th and 19th Centuries', *British Journal of Sociology*, I.

[65]  Jeremy, D. J. (1984) 'Anatomy of the British Business Elite, 1860–1980', *Business History*, XXVI.

[66] Jones, D. R. (1988) *The Origins of Civic Universities; Manchester, Leeds & Liverpool* (London).

[67] Kaelble, H. (1979–80) 'Long-Term Changes in the Recruitment of the Business Elite: Germany Compared to the U.S., Great Britain and France since the Industrial Revolution', *Journal of Social History*, XIII.

[68] —— (1981) 'Educational Opportunities and Government Policies in Europe in the Period of Industrialization', in P. Flora and A. J. Heidenheimer (eds), *The Development of Welfare States in Europe and America* (New Brunswick).

[69] —— (1981) *Historical Research on Social Mobility: Western Europe and the USA in the Nineteenth and Twentieth Centuries* (London).

[70] Kelly, T. (1981) *For Advancement of Learning: the University of Liverpool, 1881–1981* (Liverpool).

[71] Kelsall, R. K. (1955) *Higher Civil Servants in Britain from 1870 to the Present Day* (London).

[72] —— (1957) *Committee of Vice-Chancellors and Principals of the Universities of the United Kingdom. Report on an Inquiry into Applications for Admission to Universities* (London).

[73] Knights, B. (1978) *The Idea of the Clerisy in the Nineteenth Century* (Cambridge).

[74] Little, A. and Westergaard, J. (1964) 'The Trend of Class Differentials in Educational Opportunity in England and Wales', *British Journal of Sociology*, XV.

[75] Locke, R. R. (1984) *The End of the Practical Man: Entrepreneurship and Higher Education in Germany, France and Great Britain, 1880–1940* (Greenwich, Conn.)

[76] —— (1989) *Management and Higher Education since 1940: the Influence of America and Japan on West Germany, Great Britain and France* (Cambridge).

[77] Lowe, R. (1988) *Education in the Post-War Years: a Social History* (London).

[78] Lyons, F. S. L. (1979) *Culture and Anarchy in Ireland, 1890–1939* (Oxford).

[79] McClelland, V. A. (1973) *English Roman Catholics and Higher Education, 1830–1903* (Oxford).

[80] McDonald, I. J. (1967) 'Untapped Reservoirs of Talent? Social Class and Opportunities in Scottish Higher Education, 1910–1960', *Scottish Educational Studies*, I.

[81] McDowell, R. B. and Webb, D. A. (1982) *Trinity College Dublin, 1592–1952: an Academic History* (Cambridge).

[82] McPherson, A. (1972) 'The Generally Educated Scot: an Old Ideal in a Changing University Structure' in A. McPherson, D. Swift and B. Bernstein, *Eighteen-Plus: the Final Selection* (Bletchley).

[83] —— (1973) 'Selections and Survivals: a Sociology of the Ancient Scottish Universities' in R. Brown (ed.), *Knowledge, Education and Cultural Change: Papers in the Sociology of Education* (London).

[84] —— (1983) 'An Angle on the Geist: Persistence and Change in the Scottish Educational Tradition' in W. M. Humes and H. M. Paterson (eds), *Scottish Culture and Scottish Education, 1800–1980* (Edinburgh).

[85] McWilliams-Tullberg, R. (1975) *Women at Cambridge: a Men's University – though of a Mixed Type* (London).

[86] Mathew, W. M. (1966) 'The Origins and Occupations of Glasgow Students, 1740–1839', *Past and Present*, No. 33.

[87] Mayer, A. J. (1981) *The Persistence of the Old Regime: Europe to the Great War* (London).

[88] Moody, T. W. (1958) 'The Irish University Question of the Nineteenth Century', *History*, XLIII.

[89] —— and Beckett, J. C. (1959) *Queen's Belfast, 1845–1949: the History of a University* (London).

[90] Moore, L. (1991) *Bajanellas and Semilinas: Aberdeen University and the Education of Women, 1860–1920* (Aberdeen).

[91] Morgan, K. O. (1981) *Rebirth of a Nation: Wales, 1880–1980* (Oxford).

[92] Müller, D. K., Ringer, F. and Simon, B. (eds) (1987) *The Rise of the Modern Educational System: Structural Change and Social Reproduction, 1870–1920* (Cambridge). [essays on general themes by Müller, Ringer; on English higher education by Simon, R. Lowe]

[93] Pedersen, J. S. (1979) 'The Reform of Women's Secondary and Higher Education: Institutional Change and Social Values in Mid and Late Victorian England', *History of Education Quarterly*, XIX.

[94] Perkin, H. (1969) *Key Profession: the History of the Association of University Teachers* (London).

[95] —— (1969) *The Origins of Modern English Society, 1780–1880* (London).

[96] —— (1978–9) 'The Recruitment of Elites in British Society since 1800', *Journal of Social History*, XII.

[97] —— (1989) *The Rise of Professional Society: England since 1880* (London).

[98] Phillipson, N. (ed.) (1983) *Universities, Society and the Future* (Edinburgh).

[99] Piper, D. W. (ed.) (1981) *Is Higher Education Fair?* (Guildford).

[100] Pollard, S. (1989) *Britain's Prime and Britain's Decline: the British Economy, 1870–1914* (London).

[101] Price, D. T. W. (1977–90) *A History of Saint David's University College Lampeter* (2 vols, Cardiff).

[102] Raven, J. (1989) 'British History and the Enterprise Culture', *Past and Present*, No. 123.

[103] Reid, I. (1981) *Social Class Differences in Britain* (2nd edn, London).

[104] Ringer, F. K. (1978) 'The Education of Elites in Modern Europe', *History of Education Quarterly*, XVIII.

[105] —— (1979) *Education and Society in Modern Europe* (London).

[106] Roach, J. P. C. (1959–60) 'Victorian Universities and the National Intelligentsia', *Victorian Studies*, III.

[107] —— (1971) *Public Examinations in England, 1850–1900* (Cambridge).

[108] Robbins, K. (1988) *Nineteenth-Century Britain: Integration and Diversity* (Oxford).

[109] [Robbins Report] (1963) *Higher Education: Report of the Committee Appointed by the Prime Minister under the Chairmanship of Lord Robbins, 1961–63* (Report and 5 Appendices, London).

[110] Robertson, P. (1984) 'Scottish Universities and Scottish Industry, 1860–1914', *Scottish Economic and Social History*, IV.

[111] —— (1990) 'The Development of an Urban University: Glasgow, 1860–1914', *History of Education Quarterly*, XXX.

[112] Roderick, G. W. and Stephens, M. (1976) 'Scientific Studies at Oxford and Cambridge, 1850–1914', *British Journal of Educational Studies*, XXIV.

[113] Roderick, G. W. and Stephens, M. (1978) *Education and Industry in the Nineteenth Century: the English Disease?* (London).

[114] Roderick, G. W. and Stephens, M. (eds) (1981) *Where did we Go Wrong? Industrial Performance, Education and the Economy in Victorian Britain* (Lewes).

[115] Roderick, G. W. (1986–7) 'Education, Culture and Industry in Wales in the Nineteenth Century', *Welsh History Review*, XIII.

[116] Rothblatt, S. (1968) *The Revolution of the Dons: Cambridge and Society in Victorian England* (London).

[117] —— (1976) *Tradition and Change in English Liberal Education: an Essay in History and Culture* (London).

[118] —— (1987) 'Historical and Comparative Remarks on the Federal Principle in Higher Education', *History of Education*, XVI.

[119] —— (1988) 'London: a Metropolitan University?', in T. Bender (ed.) *The University and the City: from Medieval Origins to the Present* (New York).

[120] Rubinstein, W. D. (1986) 'Education and the Social Origins of British Elites, 1880–1970', *Past and Present*, No. 112. [also reprinted in Rubinstein, 1987]

[121] —— (1987) *Elites and the Wealthy in Modern British History: Essays in Social and Economic History* (Brighton).

[122] Sanderson, M. (1972) *The Universities and British Industry, 1850–1970* (London).

[123] —— (1975) *The Universities in the Nineteenth Century* (London). [a selection of source material with commentary]

[124] —— (1983) *Education, Economic Change and Society in England, 1780–1870* (London). [new edn 1991]

[125] —— (1987) *Educational Opportunity and Social Change in England* (London).

[126] —— (1988) 'The English Civic Universities and the "Industrial Spirit", 1870–1914', *Historical Research*, LXI.

[127] Scott, P. (1984) *The Crisis of the University* (London).

[128] Sherington, G. (1981) *English Education, Social Change and War, 1911–20* (Manchester).

[129] Shils, E. (1955) 'The Intellectuals. I: Great Britain', *Encounter*, IV.

[130] Shinn, C. H. (1986) *Paying the Piper: the Development of the University Grants Committee, 1919–46* (Lewes).

[131] Simon, B. (1960) *Studies in the History of Education, 1780–1870* (London). [republished 1976 as *The Two Nations and the Educational Structure, 1780–1870*]

[132] Slee, P. R. H. (1986) *Learning and a Liberal Education: the Study of Modern History in the Universities of Oxford, Cambridge and Manchester, 1800–1914* (Manchester).

[133] —— (1987) 'Professor Soffer's "History at Oxford"', *Historical Journal*, XXX.

[134] —— (1988) 'The Oxford Idea of a Liberal Education, 1800–1860: the Invention of Tradition and the Manufacture of Practice', *History of Universities*, VII.

[135] Smith, D. (1982) *Conflict and Compromise. Class Formation in English Society, 1830–1914: a Comparative Study of Birmingham and Sheffield* (London).

[136] Soffer, R. (1987) 'The Modern University and National Values, 1850–1930', *Historical Research*, LX.

[137] —— (1987) 'Nation, Duty, Character and Confidence: History at Oxford, 1850–1914', *Historical Journal*, XXX.

[138] —— (1988) 'The Development of Disciplines in the Modern English University', *Historical Journal*, XXXI.

[139] Sparrow, J. (1967) *Mark Pattison and the Idea of a University* (Cambridge).

[140] Stanworth, P. and Giddens, A. (eds) (1974) *Elites and Power in British Society* (Cambridge).

[141] Stewart, W. A. C. (1989) *Higher Education in Postwar Britain* (London).

[142] Stone, L. (ed.) (1975) *The University in Society. Volume I: Oxford and Cambridge from the 14th to the Early 19th Century* (Princeton).

[143] Sutherland, G. (1987) 'The Movement for the Higher Education of Women: its Social and Intellectual Context in England, c. 1840–80' in P. J. Waller (ed.), *Politics and Social Change in Modern Britain: Essays Presented to A. F. Thompson* (Brighton).

[144] Thompson, F. M. L. (ed.) (1990) *The University of London and the World of Learning, 1836–1986* (London).

[145] Vaughan, M. and Archer, M. S. (1971) *Social Conflict and Educational Change in England and France, 1789–1848* (Cambridge).

[146] Vicinus, M. (1985) *Independent Women: Work and Community for Single Women, 1850–1920* (London).

[147] Ward, W. R. (1965) *Victorian Oxford* (London).

[148] Wiener, M. (1981) *English Culture and the Decline of the Industrial Spirit, 1850–1980* (Cambridge).

[149] Williams, J. G. (1985) *The University College of North Wales: Foundations, 1884–1927* (Cardiff).

[150] Wright, C. J. (1979) 'Academics and their Aims: English and Scottish Approaches to University Education in the Nineteenth Century', *History of Education*, VIII.

# Index

Brief details of institutions include dates for post-1800 foundations: they are dates of opening rather than formal foundation when the two differ. Constituent technical and medical colleges, and colleges of the University of London not mentioned in the text, are not covered. C = College, UC = University College, U = University.

# New Studies in Economic and Social History

*Titles in the series available from Cambridge University Press:*

*Previously published as*

# Studies in Economic History

*Titles in the series available from the Macmillan Press Limited*

# Economic History Society

The Economic History Society, which numbers around 3,000 members, publishes the *Economic History Review* four times a year (free to members) and holds an annual conference.

Enquiries about membership should be addressed to

**The Assistant Secretary**
**Economic History Society**
**PO Box 70**
**Kingswood**
**Bristol**
**BS15 5TB**

Full-time students may join at special rates.